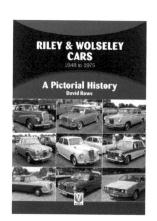

RILEY & WOLSELEY CARS
1948 to 1975

A Pictorial History
David Rowe

More great books from Veloce:

A Pictorial History - Series

Austin Cars 1948 to 1990 – A Pictorial History (Rowe)

Citroën Cars 1934 to 1986 – A Pictorial History (Parish)

Ford Cars (UK) – A Pictorial History (Rowe)

Jaguar Cars 1922 to 2005 – A Pictorial History (Greene)

Mercedes-Benz 1950 to 1998 – A Pictorial History (Greene)

Morris Cars – 1948-1984 (Newell)

Riley & Wolseley Cars of the 1950s, 1960s and 1970s – A Pictorial History (Rowe)

Rootes Cars of the 50s, 60s & 70s – Hillman, Humber, Singer, Sunbeam & Talbot, A Pictorial History (Rowe)

Rover Cars 1945 to 2005 – A Pictorial History (Taylor)

Those Were The Days ... Series

Alpine Trials & Rallies 1910-1973 (Pfundner)

American ½-ton Pickup Trucks of the 1950s (Mort)

American ½-ton Pickup Trucks of the 1960s (Mort)

American 'Independent' Automakers – AMC to Willys 1945 to 1960 (Mort)

American Station Wagons – The Golden Era 1950-1975 (Mort)

American Trucks of the 1950s (Mort)

American Trucks of the 1960s (Mort)

American Woodies 1928-1953 (Mort)

Anglo-American Cars from the 1930s to the 1970s (Mort)

Austerity Motoring (Bobbitt)

Austins, The last real (Peck)

Brighton National Speed Trials (Gardiner)

British and European Trucks of the 1970s (Peck)

British Drag Racing – The early years (Pettitt)

British Lorries of the 1950s (Bobbitt)

British Lorries of the 1960s (Bobbitt)

British Touring Car Racing (Collins)

British Police Cars (Walker)

British Woodies (Peck)

Buick Riviera (Mort)

Café Racer Phenomenon, The (Walker)

Chevrolet ½-ton C/K-Series Pickup Trucks 1973-1987 (Mort)

Don Hayter's MGB Story – The birth of the MGB in MG's Abingdon Design & Development Office (Hayter)

Drag Bike Racing in Britain – From the mid '60s to the mid '80s (Lee)

Dune Buggy Phenomenon, The (Hale)

Dune Buggy Phenomenon Volume 2, The (Hale)

Endurance Racing at Silverstone in the 1970s & 1980s (Parker)

Hot Rod & Stock Car Racing in Britain in the 1980s (Neil)

Mercedes-Benz Trucks (Peck)

MG's Abingdon Factory (Moylan)

Motor Racing at Brands Hatch in the Seventies (Parker)

Motor Racing at Brands Hatch in the Eighties (Parker)

Motor Racing at Crystal Palace (Collins)

Motor Racing at Goodwood in the Sixties (Gardiner)

Motor Racing at Nassau in the 1950s & 1960s (O'Neil)

Motor Racing at Oulton Park in the 1960s (McFadyen)

Motor Racing at Oulton Park in the 1970s (McFadyen)

Motor Racing at Thruxton in the 1970s (Grant-Braham)

Motor Racing at Thruxton in the 1980s (Grant-Braham)

Superprix – The Story of Birmingham Motor Race (Page & Collins)

Three Wheelers (Bobbitt)

Great Cars

Austin-Healey – A celebration of the fabulous 'Big' Healey (Piggott)

Jaguar E-type (Thorley)

Jaguar Mark 1 & 2 (Thorley)

Jaguar XK A Celebration of Jaguar's 1950s Classic (Thorley)

Triumph TR – TR2 to 6: The last of the traditional sports cars (Piggott)

Volkswagen Beetle – A Celebration of the World's Most Popular Car (Copping)

Veloce's other imprints offer a diverse range of general interest, animal care and children's books.

www.veloce.co.uk

First published as Wolseley Cars 1948 to 1975 (ISBN: 978-1-787110-78-6) in July 2017. New expanded edition published February 2022, reprinted September 2022 and October 2023 by Veloce Publishing Limited, Veloce House, Parkway Farm Business Park, Middle Farm Way, Poundbury, Dorchester DT1 3AR, England. Tel: (+44) 01305 260068 / Fax 01305 250479 / email info@veloce.co.uk / web www.veloce.co.uk or www.velocebooks.com.
ISBN: 978-1-787117-91-4; UPC: 6-36847-01791-0.
Typesetting, design and page make-up all by Veloce Publishing Ltd on Apple Mac. Printed and bound by CPI Group (UK) Ltd, Croydon, CR0 4YY.

RILEY & WOLSELEY CARS
1948 to 1975

A Pictorial History
David Rowe

VELOCE

CONTENTS

For full model listing, see the Index

A history of the Wolseley Car Company

Frederick Wolseley was born in 1837 in Dublin. He emigrated to Australia in 1854 and worked on a sheep station, before buying his own. He experimented with, and subsequently created, mechanised sheep-shearing equipment, and, having taking out patents to protect his inventions, then set up the Wolseley Sheep Shearing Machine Company. In 1889 he established an English company and closed down the Australian business.

Herbert Austin was born in 1866 in Yorkshire, and moved to Australia in 1884. He worked for a number of engineering firms there, before joining the Wolseley Sheep Shearing Company. Whilst working for the Wolseley company, he demonstrated his ability to improve the equipment, and, having taken out patents on the changes he had made, was given shares in the company and appointed manager of the English branch of the company based in Birmingham.

Unfortunately, having sub-contracted some of the work to local businesses, who failed to manufacture components to a satisfactory standard, Austin found the company's reputation for quality was damaged, and sales were thus disappointing. Acknowledging the growing number of bicycle manufacturing businesses springing up around Birmingham – Humber, Rover, Singer, to name but a few – Austin turned to manufacturing machine tools and components for the cycle companies, ultimately becoming an agent selling cycles for these businesses, in addition to manufacturing the parts used in their production.

In 1895, Austin visited Paris and became intrigued with a Bollée motor tricycle that he saw there, and so, upon his return to England, built his own version of this vehicle. In 1896 the directors of the Wolseley company agreed to invest money in building prototypes, and so a second three-wheeler was built and displayed at the National Cycle Exhibition at Crystal Palace. The public, however, was more interested in the four-wheeled motor cars that were beginning to appear, and so Austin produced a four-wheeler, which he drove in the 1000-mile trial organised by the Automobile Club of Great Britain in 1900, and which he

successfully completed. This car had tiller steering and a combination of belt and chain drives; later cars were equipped with wheeled steering, and belt drive was discontinued, all cars now having full chain drive.

By this time Austin had decided that the company should start producing motor cars in quantity. However, the company could not provide sufficient financial resources to Austin, and so he turned to Sir Hiram Maxim, whose company manufactured guns, and who had previously expressed an interest in producing motor cars. Maxim's company had been taken over by Vickers, the engineering conglomerate, who, although interested in the idea of producing cars, did not agree with Austin's ideas of continuing with horizontally opposed engines, while other manufacturers were turning to vertical engines. How ironic that one of the most successful cars of all time, the Volkswagen Beetle, developed some 30 years later, used a horizontally opposed engine.

In 1901, Vickers set up the Wolseley Tool and Motor Car Company at Adderley Park, Birmingham, with Austin as manager. It also acquired all of Austin's patents, and the original Wolseley Sheep-Shearing Company, which continued to produce sheep-shearing equipment, but was excluded from any involvement with motor manufacturing.

Wolseley took part in a number of racing events to promote its cars, in accordance with the philosophy 'win on Sunday, sell on Monday.' The Wolseley cars did have some success, but, with the public now turning to vertically-engined cars, sales of Wolseleys fell.

One of Wolseley's rivals in the car manufacturing business was the Siddeley Motor Car company. Founded by John Davenport Siddeley, it had originally been involved in the tyre industry, before the decision was taken to import Peugeot cars, and then subsequently to produce cars of its own. The company, however, did not have suitable premises to build cars, so it turned to Vickers in 1903, and agreed that the cars would be built in a Vickers factory in Kent. With sales of the Siddeley models rising and Wolseleys falling, Austin left the Wolseley company in 1905 to set up his own business – the Austin Motor Company, on the site of a disused printing works at Longbridge near Birmingham.

His cars would now feature vertical engines.

Following Austin's departure from Wolseley, the decision was taken to appoint Siddeley as general manager, the name of the company subsequently becoming Wolseley-Siddeley. In addition to cars, the company started manufacturing trucks and buses in 1905, and taxi-cabs were produced for a short while after 1907. John Siddeley left Wolseley in 1909, and joined the Deasey Motor Car Manufacturing Company – its cars then became Siddeley-Deasy, causing a problem for the Vickers company which was using the Wolseley-Siddeley name. This was eventually resolved in 1911, when the company was renamed Wolseley Motors Limited. By this time E Hopwood, of British Electric Traction, and A J McCormack, of Clyde Components Company, had been brought in as directors, and Wolseley was now producing a whole range of cars with different engines – some with four-cylinders and some with six cylinders – making it one of the largest car makers in the UK by 1914.

As well as cars and commercial vehicles, the Wolseley company produced engines for, amongst other things, the tracked motorised sleighs used on Scott's 1910-1913 Antarctic expedition, and a range of marine engines, some of which were used for racing. Strangest of all was a two-wheeled Gyrocar, built in 1912 for the Russian Count Schilovsky – in appearance it looked like an elongated motorcycle with bench seats, and had stabiliser wheels to keep it upright when stationary, whilst a gyroscope system kept it upright whilst moving. Although unsuccessful at first, after some development it worked satisfactorily. By 1914, however, and the onset of World War 1, the project was abandoned, and it was buried in the ground at the factory; it was dug up some years later, but subsequently scrapped in the 1940s.

Wolseley Motors had built a few aero engines prior to 1914, and assembled those of other manufacturers during the Great War. However, it is the production of a large range of lorries, utilised in many roles from ambulances to armoured cars, as well as for general load carrying, for which it will probably be remembered. These lorries could be seen around for a number of years afterwards, fulfilling many other roles. After 1918, the commercial market was flooded with ex-military vehicles, so Wolseley decided to discontinue commercial vehicle production, and concentrate on passenger cars instead, reintroducing its 1914 models until such time as it could develop new models.

Having experienced building new overhead camshaft (OHC) aero engines, Wolseley decided to incorporate this feature in some of its future car engines; at this time most car engines were of the side valve variety. In 1919, the company controlled the Ward End factory of Electric and Ordnance Accessories Company Ltd, where munitions had been made, and it raised the money to re-equip the factory for car production, giving it the potential to become the largest car company in the UK. Wolseley cars were expensive compared to the likes of Morris and other British cars, and so the company introduced a smaller 7hp model to sell alongside its other models. It also built racing versions of its cars, in an attempt to generate publicity by setting new sporting records. Unfortunately, this simply added to the costs the company was incurring by running two car factories – by 1926 the company was bankrupt, and the receivers moved in to sell off the business.

William Morris, who as well as producing his own cars had also sold Wolseley cars, was interested in acquiring the company. But he found himself in competition with, amongst others, Herbert Austin, who had been instrumental in setting up the Wolseley Car Company before leaving and successfully building up his own company. William Morris succeeded with his bid for the Wolseley company, and it ultimately became part of his Nuffield Empire in 1927. Morris saw the potential of selling his Morris cars as entry level models, and Wolseley cars as more upmarket, suitable for successful business entrepreneurs and those professionals who might otherwise have bought a Rover. I recall that for some reason Rovers used to be associated with bank managers and doctors, and Humbers with senior civil servants.

Acquiring Wolseley also provided Morris with a six-cylinder engine – all of his cars were four-cylinder. In 1930, however, Morris introduced a new Wolseley model – the Hornet. It had a tiny 1271cc six-cylinder engine, and was based

A 1935 Wolseley Hornet,
Daytona model.

on the Morris Minor, which had a four-cylinder engine. The Wolseley was also sold to specialist coachbuilders, to put their own bodywork on, and, being faster than the Morris Minor, was a popular choice. The size of the Hornet engine gradually increased over the years to 1600cc, and eventually found its way into MG cars, which were considered to be for the sporting market, whilst the Wolseley was aimed at those who preferred a little more luxury over the plainer Morris.

The illuminated radiator Wolseley badge appeared on models from 1933 onwards. All overhead camshaft engines were discontinued by the end of 1936, and all Wolseley cars were then fitted with overhead valve engines (OHV), whilst Morris cars retained side valve engines (SV). The last of the cars with an overhead camshaft, the Fourteen, became the 14/56 overhead valve model in 1937. By this time the police had started using Wolseley cars, and they can often be seen in period dramas and films.

In 1939, Wolseley launched its new small Ten car, but the onset of World War 2 meant that, once again, Wolseley found itself producing lorries and tracked vehicles for the War Department. The loss of the Ward End factory as a result of German bombing led to production of Wolseley cars being moved to

The Riley Pathfinder, introduced in 1954, had similar styling to the Wolseley 6/90 opposite, and was built on the same chassis.

Cowley in Oxford, the home of Morris Motors. At this time, Wolseley cars generally became Morris cars with better interior fittings, and their own distinctive radiator grille, they did, however, have different engines initially.

The first postwar cars were the Six-Eighty and Four-Fifty, both introduced in 1948, and based on Morris models, the Morris Six and MO models respectively. The Six-Eighty with its six-cylinder engine, and its successors the 6/99 and 6/110, were popular cars with the police. The 6/110 was often seen escorting wide loads, and they continued to be used by the police until the late 1960s.

In 1952, the Austin Motor Company merged with the Nuffield Organisation, which had taken control of Wolseley in 1927. The new combined Nuffield and Austin businesses became known as BMC (British Motor Corporation). Herbert Austin died in 1941, and since 1938 the business had been run by Leonard Lord, who had previously worked for the Nuffield Organisation, where, for a while, he had been responsible for the Wolseley Car Company.

At first, Wolseley cars continued as variants of Nuffield cars, including Riley, acquired by Morris in 1938, and MG (Morris Garages), the sporting division developed by Cecil Kimber, the manager of Morris' Oxford dealership.

Much later, following the arrival of the Farina-designed cars – the Wolseley 15/60 in 1958, then the Austin Cambridge, Morris Oxford, MG Magnette and Riley 4/68 in 1959 – Wolseley cars started to become variants of Austin cars. The Wolseley 6/99 of 1959, for instance, was an upmarket version of the Austin A99, and the Austin and Wolseley names became synonymous with each other once again.

This practice, referred to as 'badge engineering,' was also adopted by other car manufacturers, such as the Rootes Group, whose Singer cars were, after 1955, upmarket versions of Hillman cars, while its Sunbeam cars represented the sporting range: basically the same bodyshells, but with some minor styling difference (usually the radiator grille). The engines, however, although derived from the same basic engine block, were often offered in different states of tune, according to the placement of the cars within the manufacturer's range.

The Wolseley Hornet was part of the Mini range, and the 18/85 was part of the Austin and Morris 1800 range – albeit with a distinctive front grille, its traditional illuminated badge, and different rear lights. It was not until the introduction of the Austin Maxi in 1968, and Morris Marina in 1971, that the manufacturer's names started to represent different models once again. BMC (or British Motor Holdings (BMH) as it was now named) merged with the Leyland Motor Company, owners of Triumph and Rover, in 1968, and rationalisation of model names and ranges started to take place. The first casualty was Riley, which ceased to exist after 1969, followed by Wolseley and its final model, the 18/22, which was in production for less than a year in 1975. The Hornet had disappeared in 1969, when the Mini became a separate range in its own right, losing its Austin and Morris badges. In 1984 the Morris name disappeared, its final car being the Ital. From 1987 Austin cars were referred to as Austin/Rovers, with some even wearing Rover badges, and in 1994 the last of the Austin cars, the Maestro and Montego, were discontinued.

Wolseley 6/80

Introduced in October 1948, the 6/80 (or, to give it the correct name, Six-Eighty), and the similar looking 4/50 (see page 10), replaced all previous Wolseley models. The 6/80 retained its illuminated radiator badge, but saw the introduction of a two-piece divided windscreen – an unusual feature, especially given that previous Wolseleys had a more modern one-piece windscreen. The 6/80 was based on the body style of the Morris 6, but it had a more powerful six-cylinder engine with twin carburettors. This engine was an OHC unit of a completely new design, with the camshaft acting directly on the overhead valves by means of a vertical shaft, rather than the timing chain/belt arrangement associated with current engines. In 1950 the suspension was revised, and the engine compression ratio was lowered. 1951 saw the introduction of a heater as standard equipment, and in 1952 a divided front bench seat replaced the original individual seats. The model was replaced in 1954 by the 6/90.

Number produced: 24,886.
Price in 1951: £767 including Purchase Tax (introduced on 'luxury goods' from 21st October 1940 at 33.33%, VAT was introduced later, in 1973).
Standard equipment included oil pressure gauge, ammeter, clock, variable instrument lighting with dimmer switch, two glove boxes with lids, walnut-trimmed fascia and door cappings, heater, leather seats, separate front seats at launch, changed to a divided bench seat in 1952, two sun visors with mirror on passenger side (it was not unusual in the 1940s for sun visors to be optional), rear window blind, opening front and rear quarter lights, twin fog lights, reversing light, over-riders and more. Optional equipment included a radio.

COLOURS (1953): Grey metallic, Green metallic, Black.
ENGINE: Six-cylinder, OHC, bore 73.5mm, stroke 87mm, 2215cc (135.1in³), maximum bhp 72, two SU carburettors.
GEARBOX: Four-speed, steering column gear change, synchromesh on top three gears. Ratios: top 4.10, 3rd 5.51, 2nd 8.5, 1st 13.16;

Note some cars shown here have been fitted with non-standard modern indicators.

later models – top 4.555, 3rd 6.586, 2nd 10.248, 1st 14.642.
REAR AXLE: Hypoid bevel, semi-floating. Ratio: early models 4.10, later models 4.555.
BRAKES: Lockheed, front and rear 10in drums, handbrake mounted under dashboard near steering column.
STEERING: Bishop cam, adjustable telescopic column.
TYRES: 6.00 x 15, spare wheel carried in separate compartment under boot floor.
SUSPENSION: Front, independent torsion bar, rear semi-elliptic leaf springs, Armstrong hydraulic shock absorbers front and rear, later models with two telescopic shock absorbers for each front torsion bar, and one splayed shock absorber for each rear spring.
DIMENSIONS: Length 14ft 9in (4.496m); width 5ft 6in (1.676m); height 5ft 3in (1.60m); wheelbase 9ft 2in (2.794m); track front 4ft 6in (1.372m); rear 4ft 5in (1.346m); ground clearance 7in (18cm); turning circle 40ft (12.19m); kerb weight 1ton 5cwt 3qtr 16lb (1315kg), dry weight 1ton 4cwt (1220kg).*
CAPACITIES: Fuel 12 gallons (55 litres).

Right: This police car has had non-standard front and rear indicators.

Gear change diagram.

Wolseley 4/50

Introduced in 1948, the 4/50 (more correctly the Four-Fifty), along with the 6/80 (detailed above), replaced all previous Wolseley models. It is interesting to note that although the 6/80 and 4/50 were designated as upmarket versions of the Morris 6 and MO models, the 4/50 used a version of the 6/80 body, with a shorter wheelbase and bonnet to

accommodate a four-cylinder engine, whereas the 6/80 had a six-cylinder engine. Both cars were fitted with a two-piece side opening bonnet instead of the alligator style rear hinged bonnet found on the Morris 6, MO and all modern cars. The 4/50, therefore, bore little resemblance to the Morris MO, which looked more like a large Morris Minor. Further differences between the 4/50 and MO included the use of totally different engines, the Wolseley having a totally new OHC engine, whilst the MO had a smaller capacity side valve (SV) unit. Improvements for 1951 models included revised gear ratios, and, in September 1952, changes to the suspension to improve handling.

Number produced: 8925.

Price in 1950: £703 including Purchase Tax. Standard equipment included oil pressure gauge, ammeter, clock, variable instrument lighting with dimmer switch, walnut trimmed fascia, heater, leather seats, individual front seats adjustable for height and reach, two sun visors, rear window blind, opening front quarter lights, fog light fitted to nearside, reversing light and more. Note later cars have lidded glove boxes instead of open cubby holes. Optional equipment included a radio.

ENGINE: Four-cylinder, OHC, bore 73.5mm, stroke 87mm, 1476cc (90.03in^3), maximum bhp

13

Instrument layout.

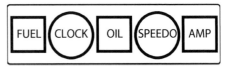

51, single SU H2 carburettor.
GEARBOX: Four-speed, steering column gear change, synchromesh on top three gears. Ratios: top 4.55, 3rd 6.83, 2nd 9.4, 1st 15.95; later models: top 4.875, 3rd 7.342, 2nd 10.98, 1st 18.56.
REAR AXLE: Hypoid bevel. Ratio early models 4.55, later models 4.875.
BRAKES: Lockheed, front and rear 9in drums. Note the 6/80 had 10in front and rear brake drums.
STEERING: Bishop cam, telescopic column adjustment.
TYRES: 5.50 x 15.
SUSPENSION: Front, independent torsion bar, rear semi-elliptic leaf springs, Armstrong hydraulic shock absorbers front and rear, later models with two Duplex telescopic shock absorbers for each front torsion bar and one splayed shock absorber for each rear spring.
DIMENSIONS: Length 14ft 1in (4.293m); width 5ft 6in (1.676m); height 5ft 3in (1.60m); wheelbase 8ft 6in (2.59m); track front and rear 4ft 5.125in (1.349m); ground clearance 7in (18cm); turning circle 38ft (11.58m); kerb weight 1ton 3cwt 2qtr (1180kg), dry weight 1ton 3cwt (1669kg).*
CAPACITIES: Fuel 9.5 gallons (43 litres).

Without badges, the 4/50 (left) and 6/80 (right) look identical.

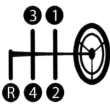

Gear change diagram.

* Note: various sources quote kerb weight as being with either a full or half a tank of fuel; unladen with approximately two gallons of fuel; dry weight is without oil, water or fuel.

Wolseley 4/44

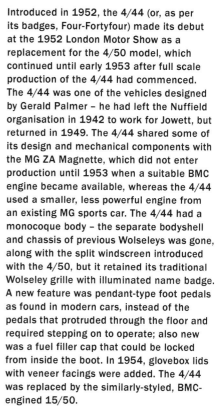

Introduced in 1952, the 4/44 (or, as per its badges, Four-Fortyfour) made its debut at the 1952 London Motor Show as a replacement for the 4/50 model, which continued until early 1953 after full scale production of the 4/44 had commenced. The 4/44 was one of the vehicles designed by Gerald Palmer – he had left the Nuffield organisation in 1942 to work for Jowett, but returned in 1949. The 4/44 shared some of its design and mechanical components with the MG ZA Magnette, which did not enter production until 1953 when a suitable BMC engine became available, whereas the 4/44 used a smaller, less powerful engine from an existing MG sports car. The 4/44 had a monocoque body – the separate bodyshell and chassis of previous Wolseleys was gone, along with the split windscreen introduced with the 4/50, but it retained its traditional Wolseley grille with illuminated name badge. A new feature was pendant-type foot pedals as found in modern cars, instead of the pedals that protruded through the floor and required stepping on to operate; also new was a fuel filler cap that could be locked from inside the boot. In 1954, glovebox lids with veneer facings were added. The 4/44 was replaced by the similarly-styled, BMC-engined 15/50.

Number produced: 29,845.

Price in 1953: £844 including Purchase Tax. Standard equipment included water temperature and oil pressure gauges, clock, instrument lighting with dimmer switch, walnut-trimmed fascia and door cappings. Glovebox lids were added in 1954, heater, leather seats, divided front bench seat with individual adjustment for each half, two sun visors (some 1950s cars had only a driver's sun visor as standard), anti-glare interior mirror, opening front and rear door quarter lights, reversing light, over-riders, wheel hub caps with 'W' motif. The spare wheel was now upright on the side of the boot, instead of in a separate compartment under the boot floor, as in the Wolseley 4/50, and this, with the petrol tank placed above the rear axle and under the rear parcel shelf, resulted in a very useful large box-shaped boot. The flush-fitting petrol fuel filler

flap was released from inside the boot, a useful anti-theft deterrent but it did mean opening the boot every time you needed to fill up. Optional equipment included radio, windscreen washers, and single or twin fog lights.

COLOURS (1953): Grey metallic, Green metallic, Black.
COLOURS (1955): Mist Grey, Connaught Green, Black, Maroon.
ENGINE: Four-cylinder, OHV, bore 66.5mm, stroke 90mm, 1250cc (76.25in³), maximum bhp 46, single SU H2 carburettor.
GEARBOX: Four-speed, steering column gear change, synchromesh on top three gears. Ratios: top 4.875, 3rd 7.342, 2nd 10.983, 1st 18.559
REAR AXLE: Hypoid bevel, semi floating.
BRAKES: Lockheed, front and rear 9in drums, handbrake mounted under the dashboard near the steering column.
STEERING: Rack and pinion.
TYRES: 5.50 x 15.
SUSPENSION: Front, coil spring and wishbone,

Instrument layout.

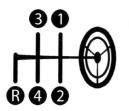

Gear change diagram.

rear semi-elliptic leaf springs, Girling telescopic shock absorbers front and rear.
DIMENSIONS: Length 14ft 5in (4.394m); width 5ft 1in (1.55m); height 5ft 0in (1.52m); wheelbase 8ft 5in (2.59m); track front 4ft 2.69in (1.287m); rear 4ft 3in (1.295m); ground clearance 7in (18cm); turning circle 36ft (10.97m); unladen weight 1ton 2cwt 1qtr (1130kg).*
CAPACITIES: Fuel 9.5 gallons (43 litres).

17

Wolseley 15/50

The Fifteen-Fifty introduced in June 1956 was, in effect, a better equipped 4/44 with a new BMC engine, as used in the MG ZA/ZB saloons to which it appeared very similar. This engine, referred to as the 'B series,' gradually increased in size over a number of years from 1489cc to 1622cc, and eventually 1798cc, for use in the MGB sports car. Externally the 15/50 can be identified by its long, slightly curved chrome strip across both doors, whereas the 4/44 had a short straight strip on the front doors only. It is interesting to note that the 15/50 boot lid badges were initially in the same style as the 4/44, but changed to a smaller script with the Wolseley name above it on later saloons. Compare the Champagne car on the right with the Maroon car at the bottom of this page. Other differences between the 4/44 and 15/50 included a change from column gear change to floor-mounted for the 15/50. The handbrake remained under the dashboard – a feature commonly found in cars during the 1950s, as, together with column gear change and front bench seats, it allowed three people to sit in the front of the car, although not very practical if the car was rather narrow (perhaps that's why early car brochures, with artwork instead of photographs, often had disproportionately small people drawn in them). Manumatic automatic transmission became available in late 1956.

Number produced: 12,352.

Price in 1956: £961 including Purchase Tax. Standard equipment included water temperature and oil pressure gauges, clock, walnut-trimmed fascia, glovebox lids and door cappings, heater, leather seats, divided front bench seat with individual adjustment for each half, two sun visors, arm rests on rear doors, children's safety locking on all doors, anti-glare interior mirror, windscreen washers, opening front door quarter lights (note the 4/44 had opening quarter lights on both front and rear doors), reversing light, twin fog lights (optional on 4/44), over-riders, spare wheel situated vertically on left side of boot, with a comprehensive tool kit in recess on right. Optional equipment included radio,

Instrument layout.

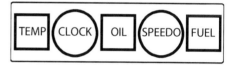

Manumatic automatic transmission, wheel rim embellishers.

COLOURS (1958): Yukon Grey, Birch Grey, Alhambra Green, Black, Maroon, Champagne.
ENGINE: Four-cylinder, OHV, bore 73.025mm, stroke 89mm, 1489cc (90.88in^3), maximum bhp 50, single SU H2 carburettor.
GEARBOX: Four-speed, floor-mounted gear change, synchromesh on top three gears. Ratios, manual and Manumatic, top 4.875, 3rd 6.698, 2nd 10.793, 1st 17.745
REAR AXLE: Hypoid bevel, three quarter floating.
BRAKES: Lockheed, front and rear 9in drums, handbrake mounted under dashboard near the steering column.
STEERING: Rack and pinion.
TYRES: 5.60 x 15.
SUSPENSION: Front, coil spring and wishbone, rear semi-elliptic leaf springs, Armstrong or Girling telescopic shock absorbers front and rear.
DIMENSIONS: Length 14ft 5in (4.394m); width 5ft 1in (1.549m); height 5ft 0in (1.524m);

Note, the car above has been fitted with non-standard flashing indicators – a popular modification to older cars.

Riley & Wolseley Cars 1948 to 1975 – A Pictorial History

Gear change diagram. Cars equipped with Manumatic had the same gear lever arrangement but instead of a clutch pedal they had a button on top of the gear lever which was pressed down whilst changing gear.

wheelbase 8ft 6in (2.591m); track front 4ft 2.69in (1.288m); rear 4ft 3in (1.295m); ground clearance 7.25in (18.4cm); turning circle 36ft (10.97m); unladen weight 1ton 1cwt 3qtr (1204kg).*

CAPACITIES: Fuel 9.25 gallons (42 litres).

Wolseley 6/90 series 1

Introduced in 1954 to replace the 6/80, the Six-Ninety shared some of its styling with the Riley Pathfinder that had been introduced in 1953. However, this role was later reversed, with the Riley 2.6 being based on the 6/90 series 3. The original idea had been that Gerald Palmer would design two large cars, a Riley and a Wolseley, and two medium sized cars, an MG and a Wolseley. This would have created four different bodyshells, so the decision was taken that only two basic cars would be built, but that each car would use different engines, and have some minor styling differences to identify them as individual models. However, whereas the smaller 4/44 introduced in 1952 had a monocoque body, the 6/90 has a traditional chassis with separate body. The 6/90 series 1 had a plastic instrument panel instead of the usual wooden dashboard, and coil rear springs instead of the semi-elliptic leaf springs that most cars of the era used. It was fitted with the new six-cylinder overhead valve BMC engine referred to as the C-series – the engine that would go on to power the Austin Healey 100-Six sports car in 1956, and eventually, in enlarged 2912cc form, the MG MGC in 1967. The Riley, however, retained the engine used in its RM series, and had its gear change on the right-hand side of the driver's seat.

Number produced: 5776.

Price in 1954: £1205 including Purchase Tax.

Standard equipment included water temperature and oil pressure gauges, ammeter, clock, heater, leather upholstery, divided front bench seat, windscreen washers, fog lights, reversing light, over-riders and more. Optional equipment included a radio.

COLOURS (1954): Connaught Green, Mist Grey, Maroon, Black.

ENGINE: Six-cylinder, OHV, bore 79.375mm, stroke 88.9mm, 2639cc (161in³), maximum bhp 95, two SU H4 carburettors.

GEARBOX: Four-speed, steering column gear change, synchromesh on top three gears.

Ratios: top 4.10, 3rd 5.883, 2nd 8.446, 1st 13.591.

REAR AXLE: Hypoid bevel, three quarter floating.

BRAKES: Lockheed, front and rear 11in drums, handbrake mounted under dashboard near the steering column.

STEERING: Bishop cam, telescopically adjustable steering column.

TYRES: 6.00 x 15, spare wheel in carrier underneath the rear of the car.

SUSPENSION: Front, torsion bar, wishbones and links, rear coil springs and Panhard rod, telescopic hydraulic dampers front and rear.

DIMENSIONS: Length 15ft 8in (4.775m); width 5ft 7in (1.702m); height 5ft 2in (1.575m); wheelbase 9ft 5.5in (2.883m); track front 4ft 6.375in (1.381m); rear 4ft 6.5in (1.384m); ground clearance 7in (17.78cm); turning circle 37ft 3in (11.35m); unladen weight 1ton 10cwt (1524kg) approximately, dry weight 1ton 9cwt 1qtr (1487kg).*

CAPACITIES: Fuel 13 gallons (59 litres). Boot 11ft³ (0.3m³).

Left: Rear lights for 6/90 mark 1. Note the additional non-standard light, compared with the light unit shown for series 2 and 3 on the right.

Gear change diagram. Note reverse is now nearer the steering wheel – on the 6/80 it was nearest to the dashboard.

Wolseley 6/90 series 2

The Six-Ninety series 2 was introduced in October 1956 to replace the series 1, and had a very short production run of only eight months. Its predecessor, introduced in the autumn of 1954, was in production for two years before it was discontinued. New for the series 2 was the reintroduction of a wooden dashboard and semi-elliptic rear leaf springs. It had different rear lights to series 1, but the rear window remained the same size (it was enlarged for the series 3, making it simple to visually identify the three different models). A Riley style gear change on the right-hand side of the driver's seat replaced the steering column gear change of the series 1.

Number produced: 1024.

Price in 1956: £806 plus £404 Purchase Tax, giving a total of £1210.

Standard equipment included water temperature and oil pressure gauges, ammeter, clock, variable instrument lighting switch, heater, leather seats, divided front bench seat with individual adjustment for each half, windscreen washers, opening front door quarter lights, fog lights, reversing light, over-riders. New for the series 2 was a key operated lockable fuel filler flap, centre folding armrest in rear seat and walnut finish

dashboard with lockable glovebox. Optional equipment included radio and, new for the series 2 models, overdrive or automatic transmission.

COLOURS (1956): Alhambra Green, Swiss Grey, Yukon Grey, Champagne Beige, Maroon, Black.
ENGINE: Six-cylinder, OHV, bore 79.375mm, stroke 88.9mm, 2639cc (161in^3), maximum bhp 95, two SU H4 carburettors.
GEARBOX: Four-speed, floor-mounted on right-hand side of driver's seat, synchromesh on top three gears. Ratios: top 4.10, 3rd 5.883, 2nd 8.446, 1st 13.591
REAR AXLE: Hypoid bevel, three quarter floating.
BRAKES: Lockheed, front and rear 11in drums.
STEERING: Bishop cam, telescopically adjustable steering column.
TYRES: 6.00 x 15, spare wheel in carrier under the floor at the rear of the car which although it was exposed to mud and water from the road meant that changing wheels in the event of a puncture did not result in having to place a dirty wheel back in the boot.
SUSPENSION: Front, torsion bar, wishbones and links, rear semi-elliptic leaf springs, telescopic hydraulic dampers front and rear.
DIMENSIONS: Length 15ft 8in (4.775m); width 5ft 7in (1.702m); height 5ft 2in (1.575m); wheelbase 9ft 5.5in (2.883m); track front 4ft 6.375in (1.381m); rear 4ft 6.5in (1.384m); ground clearance 7in (17.78cm); turning circle 37ft 3in (11.35m); unladen weight 1ton 10cwt (1524kg) approximately, dry weight 1ton 9cwt 1qtr (1487kg).*
CAPACITIES: Fuel 13 gallons (59 litres). Boot 11ft^3 (0.3m^3).

Instrument layout.

Gear change diagram. The gear change was fitted next to the right-hand side of the driver's seat, with a section of the seat base removed to fit around it, instead of reducing the width of the whole seat.

Compare the size of the rear windows of the 6/90 series 2 on the left with the 6/90 series 3 on the right.

Wolseley 6/90 series 3

The series 3, introduced in May 1957, featured an enlarged rear window, servo-assisted brakes and hand-operated headlight dipswitch, at a time when most cars still had the dipswitch on the floor. Later models had a smaller script Wolseley 6/90 badge on boot lid instead of the large 6/90 numbers, and were available with a two-tone paint finish. Export cars were fitted with flashing indicators instead of semaphore trafficators, but some UK cars such as the Maroon/Champagne Beige car included in this section can be found with flashing indicators, possibly retro-fitted. The 6/90 was replaced by the Farina-styled 6/99 in July 1959, some seven months after the 15/50 had been replaced by the Farina-styled 15/60. The Six-Ninety, like its predecessor the Six-Eighty, was popular with the police force, and they can be sometimes seen in films covering the 1950s period.
Number produced: 5052.
Prices in 1957: manual model £1205, automatic £1434, both including Purchase Tax.
Standard equipment included water temperature and oil pressure gauges, ammeter, clock, variable instrument lighting, walnut fascia, glovebox lids and door cappings, heater, leather seats, divided front bench seat with separate folding central armrests for each front seat, central folding armrest for rear seat, windscreen washers, opening front door quarter lights, fog lights, reversing light, over-riders, wheel rim embellishers, locking fuel filler flap, comprehensive tool kit and more. Optional equipment included radio, overdrive or automatic transmission, Duotone paint finish.
COLOURS (1958): Single tones, Alhambra Green, Swiss Grey, Yukon Grey, Champagne Beige, Maroon, Black. Duotones (roof colour

Instrument layout. Note cars can be found with the speedometer on the right or left-hand side.

Note the grey car above has the early simple type 6/90 badge, whereas the Maroon/Champagne Beige car below has the later Wolseley 6/90 script.

first), Island Green/Alhambra Green, Maroon/ Champagne Beige, Black/Birch Grey, Yukon Grey/Birch Grey, Old English White/Yukon Grey.
ENGINE: Six-cylinder, OHV, bore 79.375mm, stroke 88.9mm, 2639cc (161in^3), maximum bhp 95, two SU H4 carburettors.
GEARBOX: Four-speed, floor-mounted on right-hand side of driver's seat, synchromesh on top three gears. Ratios: top 4.10, 3rd 5.883, 2nd 8.446, 1st 13.591.
REAR AXLE: Hypoid bevel, three quarter floating.

BRAKES: Lockheed, front and rear 11in drums – these were now 3in wide, series 1 and 2 were 2.4in. Also new for the series 3 was servo power assistance. The handbrake remained under the dashboard near the steering column.
STEERING: Bishop cam, telescopically adjustable steering column.
TYRES: 6.40 x 15.
SUSPENSION: Front, torsion bar, wishbones and links, rear semi-elliptic leaf springs, telescopic hydraulic dampers front and rear.
DIMENSIONS: Length 15ft 8in (4.775m); width 5ft 7in (1.702m); height 5ft 2in (1.57m); wheelbase 9ft 5.5in (2.883m); track front 4ft 6.375in (1.381m); rear 4ft 6.5in (1.384m); ground clearance 7in (17.78cm); turning circle 37ft 3in (11.35m); unladen weight 1ton 10cwt (1524kg) approximately, dry weight 1ton 9cwt 1qtr (1487kg).*
CAPACITIES: Fuel 13 gallons (59 litres). Boot 11ft³ (0.3m³).

Note, the former police car on the left has lights fitted above radiator and boot signs to illuminate them at night.

Left, manual gear change diagram; right, automatic.

Comparison sales figures:		
6/80	25,281	(1948-1954)
6/90	11,852	(1954-1959)
6/99	13,108	(1959-1961)
6/110	29,101	(1961-1968)

* Note: various sources quote kerb weight as being with either a full or half a tank of fuel; unladen with approximately two gallons of fuel; dry weight is without oil, water or fuel.

Wolseley 1500 mark 1

The Fifteen Hundred was introduced in April 1957, a few months ahead of its counterpart, the Riley One-Point-Five. As is often the case with Wolseley cars, perhaps because so few of them had model names, the full title is usually abbreviated, and thus this car is affectionately known as the 1500. The 1500 was initially conceived as a replacement for the Morris Minor, designed by Alec Issigonis, that had been introduced in 1948. The Minor, ironically, stayed in production until late 1970, five years after the 1500 was discontinued in September 1965. The Minor Traveller estate continued for an additional year until November 1971. The finalised styling of the 1500 was carried out by Dick Burzi, but, when it was later replaced by another Issigonis model, the 1100/1300, the styling was influenced by the Italian company Pininfarina. Initially, the 1500 was to have been fitted with a 1200cc version of the BMC B-series engine, but the decision was subsequently taken to have a 1500cc engine fitted, this engine would then go on to be fitted in the Wolseley 15/60 introduced in 1958.

Number produced: 46,438 (the mark 1 which had a three-year run, outsold the mark 3 which was produced for four years.)

Gear change diagram. Note, unlike many Wolseleys before and after, the 1500 was never offered with an automatic option or overdrive.

Price when introduced: £759.
A Fleet model was introduced in 1959, at which point the original 1500 became known as the Family model. The Fleet model was only available in a single tone paint finish, had cloth instead of leather seats, and no wood trim.
Standard equipment for the Family model included water temperature and oil pressure gauges, wood-trimmed fascia and door cappings, two gloveboxes, leather seats, adjustable individual front bucket seats, two sun visors, anti-glare mirror, opening front

door quarter lights, over-riders, illuminated radiator badge and more. Optional equipment included heater, radio, windscreen washers, Duotone paint scheme.

COLOURS (1958): Maroon, Champagne, Yukon Grey, Black, Alhambra Green, Island Green. Duotones, lower body colour and roof first: Maroon/Champagne, Yukon Grey/Off White, Black/Champagne, Black/Island Green, Alhambra Green/Island Green, Island Green/Off White.

ENGINE: Four-cylinder, OHV, bore 73.02mm, stroke 88.9mm, 1489cc, (90.88in^3), maximum bhp 50, single SU H2 carburettor (1957-1958), SU HS2 carburettor from 1959.

GEARBOX: Four-speed, floor-mounted gear change, synchromesh on top three gears. Ratios: top 3.73, 3rd 5.12, 2nd 8.25, 1st 13.56.

REAR AXLE: Hypoid bevel, three quarter floating.

BRAKES: Lockheed front 9in and rear 8in drums, handbrake between front seats, earlier

Instrument layout.

Front end styles: left, mark 1 and 2; right, mark 3.

Wolseley cars had the handbrake under the dashboard.

STEERING: Rack and pinion.

TYRES: 5.00 x 14; from May 1959, 5.60 x 14.

SUSPENSION: Front, torsion bars with vernier adjustment, swivel pins, rear, semi-elliptic leaf springs, lever arm shock absorbers front and rear, note some vehicles may have been fitted with rear anti-roll bar and telescopic shock absorbers, instead of lever arm type to improve handling characteristics.

DIMENSIONS: Length 12ft 7.75in (3.854m); width 5ft 1in (1.549m); height 4ft 11.75in (1.518m); wheelbase 7ft 2in (2.184m); track front 4ft 2.9in (1.293m); rear 4ft 2.3in (1.278m); ground clearance 6.5in (16.5cm); turning circle 34ft (10.363m); unladen weight 18cwt 1qtr 16lb (934kg).

CAPACITIES: Fuel 7 gallons (32 litres). Boot 12.5ft^3 (0.32m^3).

The green mark 1 car below has been painted in the same style as the mark 2 cars.

Wolseley 1500 mark 2

Introduced in May 1960, the Fifteen Hundred mark 2 now had hidden bonnet and boot hinges, and revised side trim. The Duotone paint scheme was changed from the style used on the mark 1, where the cars had a contrasting colour for the middle section, to a simpler style, where the cars had the lower and upper half painted in different colours. From the early 1960s, many manufacturers painted the body in one colour and the roof in another, as seen on the Hornet; however, Wolseley reverted to the three section style for its 1100 range.

Number produced: 22,295.
Price in 1961: £803.

Standard equipment included water temperature and oil pressure gauges, wood-trimmed fascia and door cappings, two gloveboxes, leather seats, adjustable individual front bucket seats, two sun visors, anti-glare mirror, opening front door quarter lights, over-riders, illuminated radiator badge, new was a full width parcel shelf under the dashboard. Optional equipment included heater, radio, windscreen washers and more.

COLOURS (1960): Maroon, Yukon Grey, Smoke Grey, Black, Vale Green. Duotones,

Gear change diagram.

lower body colour first: Maroon/Whitehall Beige, Yukon Grey/Birch Grey, Vale Green/Island Green, Navy Blue/Smoke Grey.

ENGINE: Four-cylinder, OHV, bore 73.02mm, stroke 88.9mm, 1489cc (90.88in^3), maximum bhp 50, single SU HS2 carburettor.

GEARBOX: Four-speed, floor-mounted gear change, synchromesh on top three gears. Ratios: top 3.73, 3rd 5.12, 2nd 8.25, 1st 13.56.

REAR AXLE: Hypoid bevel, three quarter floating.

BRAKES: Lockheed front 9in and rear 8in drums, handbrake between front seats.

STEERING: Rack and pinion.

TYRES: 5.60 x 14, spare wheel in separate compartment under boot floor.

SUSPENSION: Front, torsion bars with vernier adjustment, swivel pins, rear, semi-elliptic leaf springs, lever arm shock absorbers front & rear.

DIMENSIONS: Length 12ft 7.75in (3.854m); width 5ft 1in (1.549m); height 4ft 11.75in (1.518m); wheelbase 7ft 2in (2.184m); track front 4ft 2.9in (1.293m); rear 4ft 2.3in

(1.278m); ground clearance 6.5in (16.5cm); turning circle 34ft (10.363m); unladen weight 18cwt 1qtr 16lb (934kg).
CAPACITIES: Fuel 7 gallons (32 litres). Boot 12.5ft^3 (0.32m^3).

Rear light arrangement: left, mark 1 and 2; right, mark 3.

Wolseley 1500 mark 3

The mark 3 arrived in October 1961, featuring revised frontal treatment with amber front indicators, and full width grille: the rear lights were also changed to a larger size. The side trim, however, remained unchanged, as did the style of the Duotone paint scheme. It can still be easily distinguished from earlier

Instrument layout.

models, although the Fifteen Hundred never carried mark 2 or 3 badges on the rear boot lid, as was a common practice in the 1960s to help identify the latest models. Later mark 3 cars featured a heater and screen washers as standard. It was discontinued in September 1965, and replaced by the Wolseley 1100.
Number produced: 31,989.
Price when introduced in 1962: £665.
Standard equipment as per mark 2, plus heater and windscreen washers for later models. Dealer-fitted accessories included radio, seat belts, anti-mist rear window panel (a popular accessory before heated rear windows), wing mirrors, fog and driving lights, locking petrol cap, roof rack and more.

COLOURS (1961): Maroon, Birch Grey, Mineral Blue, Iris Blue, Alamo Beige, Pale Ivory, Porcelain Green. Duotones, lower body colour first: Alamo Beige/Pale Ivory, Mineral Blue/Iris Blue, Damask Red/Birch Grey.

ENGINE: Four-cylinder, OHV, bore 73.02mm, stroke 88.9mm, 1489cc, (90.88in^3), maximum bhp 50, single SU HS2 carburettor.

GEARBOX: Four-speed, floor-mounted gear change, synchromesh on top three gears. Ratios: top 3.73, 3rd 5.12, 2nd 8.25, 1st 13.56.

REAR AXLE: Hypoid bevel, three quarter floating.

BRAKES: Lockheed front 9in and rear 8in drums, handbrake between front seats.

STEERING: Rack and pinion.

TYRES: 5.60 x 14.

SUSPENSION: Front, torsion bars with vernier adjustment, swivel pins, rear, semi-elliptic leaf springs, lever arm shock absorbers front & rear.

DIMENSIONS: Length 12ft 7.75in (3.854m); width 5ft 1in (1.549m); height 4ft 11.75in (1.518m); wheelbase 7ft 2in (2.184m); track front 4ft 2.9in (1.293m); rear 4ft 2.3in (1.278m); ground clearance 6.5in (16.5cm); turning circle 34ft (10.363m); unladen weight 18cwt 1qtr 16lb (934kg).

CAPACITIES: Fuel 7 gallons (32 litres). Boot 12.5ft^3 (0.32cm^3).

Gear change diagram.

Wolseley Hornet mark 1

Introduced in October 1961, this was, in effect, a luxury Mini with a boot. The design changes were made by Dick Burzi, who had designed, amongst other things, the famous 'flying A' bonnet motif for Austin cars in the 1950s. It was also the second Issigonis-derived car he had worked on. It had a central oval instrument panel, with the speedometer in the middle, oil pressure and water temperature gauges either side of it, and a walnut trim surround. It also featured additional equipment such as a heater and bonnet lock as standard. The front grille was attached to the bonnet – ideally placed for hitting your head whilst working on the engine, or just simply checking the oil level. The rear boot lid also came in for criticism, as it was hinged at the top and prone to falling down. This was first ever front-wheel drive Wolseley, but it took its Hornet name from a 1930s model. **Note**: Many sources of information for Hornet, Elf, 1100 and 1300 models list the front suspension as independent with wishbones. Here it is presented as per the manufacturer's brochures. Please note, though, that Austin/Morris 1100/1300 brochures quote suspension differently to Wolseley/Riley 1100/1300 brochures, which are exactly as per those other sources, and as used here. It is possible that 'wishbone' is a generic term to cover 'unequal levers' and 'upper and lower suspension arms.'

Number produced: 3166.

Price in 1961: £672.

Standard equipment included water temperature and oil pressure gauges, walnut-trimmed instrument panel, full width front parcel shelf, heater, leather seats, large front door bins, cubby box with ashtray either side of rear seat, protective door kick plates, windscreen washers, carpeted boot, wheel embellishers, over-riders. Optional equipment included radio, seat belts, wing mirrors, fog, spot and reversing lights.

COLOURS (1961): Main body colour first, roof second: Pale Ivory/Damask Red, Island Green/Old English White, Birch Grey/Yukon Grey, Yukon Grey/Old English White, Whitehall Beige/

Instrument layout.

Florentine Blue, Iris Blue/Old English White.
ENGINE: Four-cylinder, OHV, bore 62.94mm, stroke 68.26mm, 848cc ($51.8in^3$), maximum bhp 34, single SU HS2 carburettor.
GEARBOX: Four-speed, floor-mounted gear change, synchromesh on top three gears. Ratios: top 3.765, 3rd 5.317, 2nd 8.176, 1st 13.657. Front-wheel drive with helical spur gears and open drive shafts with universal joints, final drive ratio 3.765:1.
BRAKES: Lockheed front and rear 7in drums with handbrake between the front seats. (Some 1960s cars had the handbrake between the driver's seat and door, so you could put the car into gear with one hand while releasing the handbrake with the other. It did, of course, mean that as you released the clutch pedal you had no hands on the steering wheel, but it did make for impressive getaways.)
STEERING: Rack and pinion.
TYRES: 5.20 x 10.
SUSPENSION: Front independent with upper and lower suspension arms, rear trailing arms, with Moulton rubber cone springs and hydraulic telescopic shock absorbers front and rear.
DIMENSIONS: Length 10ft 8.75in (3.27m); width 4ft 7in (1.397m); height 4ft 5in (1.346m); wheelbase 6ft 8in (2.03m); track front 4ft 7.5in (1.41m); rear 4ft 5in (1.34m); ground clearance 6.125in (1.56cm); note, figures vary according to source, turning circle 31ft 7in (9.63m); unladen weight 12cwt 1qtr 21lb (632kg), dry weight 11cwt 3qtr (712kg).
CAPACITIES: Fuel 5.5 gallons (25 litres). Boot $6ft^3$ ($0.17m^3$).

Wolseley Hornet mark 2

Introduced in March 1963, the mark 2 had an enlarged engine of 998cc achieved by increasing both the bore and stroke, although it only gained an extra 4bhp. Externally, only a mark 2 badge on the boot lid differentiated it from the mark 1. The boot lid was now counterbalanced to offset complaints about it not staying open – not a problem experienced with the

Fifty seven convertibles were given away by Heinz as a prize in a competition and they came with an insulated food cabinet, picnic hamper, etc. Like many cars in the 1960s the conversion to convertible was done by Crayford engineering.

Mini, with its boot lid hinged at the bottom so it simply stayed down when open. Other improvements included the fitting of wider front brake drums, now 1.5in instead of 1.25in, a new diaphragm spring clutch, and combined starter/ignition arrangement instead of a separate floor-mounted starter button. Hydrolastic suspension followed in September 1964, replacing the rubber cone suspension of earlier cars.

Number produced: 16,785 – sales were more than Hornet mark 1 and 3 combined.

Price in 1963: £556.

Standard equipment for the saloon models included water temperature and oil pressure gauges, walnut-trimmed instrument panel, full width front parcel shelf, heater, leather seats, large front door bins, cubby box with ashtray either side of rear seat, protective door kick plates, windscreen washers, carpeted boot, over-riders. Optional equipment fitted by dealers included radio, seat belts, wing mirrors, fog, spot and reversing lights, external sun visor and more.

COLOURS (1964): Main body colour first, second is roof, Toga White/Damask Red, Island Green/Toga White, Birch Grey/Yukon Grey, Glen Green/Spruce Green, Maroon/Toga White, Toga White/Trafalgar Blue.

ENGINE: Four-cylinder, OHV, bore 64.58mm, stroke 76.2mm, 998cc (60.89in^3), maximum bhp 38, single SU HS2 carburettor.

GEARBOX: Four-speed, floor-mounted gear

change, synchromesh on top three gears. Ratios: top 3.765, 3rd 5.317, 2nd 8.176, 1st 13.657. Front-wheel drive with helical spur gears and open drive shafts with universal joints, final drive ratio 3.765:1.

Note, the new 998cc engine was derived from the 1100 model's engine, rather than being a development of the original 848cc unit.

BRAKES: Lockheed front and rear 7in drums, front brakes now with twin leading shoes.

STEERING: Rack and pinion.

TYRES: 5.20 x 10.

SUSPENSION: Front independent with upper and lower suspension arms, rear trailing arms, with rubber cone springs and telescopic shock absorbers (mark 1 and early mark 2), then from 1964 interconnected Hydrolastic displacers replaced the rubber cone suspension (later mark 2 and all mark 3 models).

DIMENSIONS: Length 10ft 8.75in (3.27m); width 4ft 7in (1.397m); height 4ft 5in (1.346m); wheelbase 6ft 8in (2.03m); track front 4ft 7.5in (1.41m); rear 4ft 5in (1.34m); ground clearance 6.125in (1.56cm); turning circle 31ft 7in (9.63m); unladen weight 12cwt 1qtr 21lb (632kg), dry weight 11cwt 3qtr (716kg).

CAPACITIES: Fuel 5.5 gallons (25 litres). Boot 6ft^3 (0.17m^3).

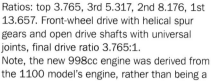

Above, manual gear change diagram; right, automatic gear change.

Wolseley Hornet mark 3

The mark 3 was introduced in October 1966, and restyled with hidden door hinges and wind-down front windows. Inside, new features were a remote floor gear change, and multi-purpose stalk on the steering column that controlled indicators, horn, headlight flasher, and high/low beam. It is easy to forget, when you are driving a modern car, that 1960s cars generally had a dipswitch on the floor, the horn either had a button in the centre of the steering wheel, or was in the form of a large ring that was easy to operate using your thumbs, and the indicator switch was usually on the right-hand side of the steering column. The optional extras list was extended for the mark 3, and now included reclining front seats, automatic transmission, and a heated rear window. The

Riley & Wolseley Cars 1948 to 1975 – A Pictorial History

Hornet was discontinued in 1969 when the Riley Elf – and, indeed, the entire Riley range – was discontinued.
Number produced: 8504.
Price in 1966: £629.
Standard equipment included water temperature and oil pressure gauges, walnut-trimmed instrument panel, full width front parcel shelf, heater, leather seats, front door bins (revised for mark 3), cubby box with ashtray either side of rear seat, protective door kick plates, windscreen washers, carpeted boot, wheel embellishers, over-riders. Optional equipment included radio, reclining front seats, seat belts, electrically heated rear window, automatic transmission, wing mirrors, auxiliary lights, roof rack.

ENGINE: Four-cylinder, OHV, bore 64.58mm, stroke 76.2mm, 998cc (60.89in^3), maximum bhp 38, single SU HS2 carburettor.
GEARBOX: Four-speed, floor-mounted gear change, synchromesh on top three gears early cars, synchromesh on all forward gears later cars. Ratios with manual gearbox, top 3.765, 3rd 5.317, 2nd 8.176, 1st 13.657; with optional automatic: top 3.765, 3rd 5.482, 2nd 6.971, 1st 10.129. Note, final drive ratio with either gearbox 3.765.
BRAKES: Lockheed front and rear 7in drums.
STEERING: Rack and pinion.

Instrument layout.

TYRES: 5.20 x 10. Note, spare wheel for all the Hornet models was in a recess under the rear boot carpet, requiring the entire contents of the boot to be removed before it could be accessed, earlier Wolseleys had the spare wheel either to the side of the boot, or in a separate compartment underneath the boot floor. Also under the carpet was the battery, not very convenient if you needed to connect jump leads to start the car.

SUSPENSION: Front independent with upper and lower suspension arms, rear trailing arms with interconnected Hydrolastic displacers front and rear.

DIMENSIONS: Length 10ft 8.75in (3.27m); width 4ft 7in (1.397m); height 4ft 5in (1.346m); wheelbase 6ft 8in (2.03m); track front 4ft 7.5in (1.41m); rear 4ft 5in (1.34m); ground clearance 6.125in (1.56cm); turning circle 31ft 7in (9.63m); unladen weight 12cwt 1qtr 21lb (632kg), dry weight 11cwt 3qtr (711kg).

CAPACITIES: Fuel 5.5 gallons (25 litres). Boot 6ft³ (0.17m³).

Note, car on the left has been fitted with a stick on rear screen heater, a popular accessory before heated rear windows became standard equipment.

41

Wolseley 1100 mark 1

Introduced in October 1965 in 1100 form, this was an upmarket version of the Austin/Morris 1100 that was launched three years earlier. The 1100/1300, although fitted with the traditional Wolseley illuminated radiator badge, never had 'Eleven Hundred' or 'Thirteen Hundred' badges on the boot lid like the Fifteen Hundred they replaced; they simply had the numbers – 1100 or 1300. The Hornet had changed to using the Hydrolastic suspension system developed by Alex Moulton, and so this system was fitted to the 1100. It consists of interconnected front and rear displacer units on each side, which, when a wheel passes over an uneven surface, causes rubber cups in the unit to come together, squeezing fluid along pipes to the opposite end of the car, keeping the car level, and eliminating the bounce effect associated with conventional springs. The spare wheel was under a panel in the boot, requiring all luggage to be removed to access it. Unlike the Hornet, the battery was under the bonnet with the engine.

Price in 1965: £754.

Standard equipment at launch included, walnut-veneered dashboard, glovebox with lid on passenger side, full width front parcel shelf and pockets in front doors, heater, windscreen washers, opening quarter lights in front doors, over-riders. Unlike earlier Wolseleys an oil pressure gauge was not provided. Optional equipment included, radio, seat belts, auxiliary lights, full wheel trims, Duotone colours, and, from May 1966, reclining front seats. Note radio, seat belts, wing mirrors and auxiliary lights were fitted at the dealership not the factory.

Glen Green/Spruce Green appear to have been the most popular colours judging by the number of cars that appear at shows. Farina Grey/Trafalgar Blue being the second most popular. These colour combinations were exclusive to Wolseley models.

ENGINE: Four-cylinder, OHV, bore 64.58mm, stroke 83.72mm, 1098cc ($67.02in^3$), maximum bhp 55, two SU HS2 carburettors.
GEARBOX: Four-speed, floor-mounted gear change, synchromesh on top three gears. Ratios: top 4.133, 3rd 5.83, 2nd 8.98, 1st 14.99. Front-wheel drive with helical spur gears, and open drive shafts with universal joints. Final drive ratio 4.133:1.
BRAKES: Lockheed, with pressure-limiting valve fitted to apportion braking more

Instrument layout.

Manual gear change diagram.

Rear light arrangements: left, earliest cars; right, later cars.

accurately between front and rear wheels, front 8in discs and rear 8in drums, handbrake between front seats.
STEERING: Rack and pinion.
TYRES: 5.50 x 12.
SUSPENSION: Front independent wishbone, rear independent trailing arms and anti-roll bar, front and rear interconnected Hydrolastic displacers.
DIMENSIONS: Length 12ft 2.75in (3.73m); width 5ft 0.4in (1.534m); height 4ft 4.7in (1.34m); wheelbase 7ft 9.5in (2.375m); track front 4ft 3.5in (1.308m); rear 4ft 2.9in (1.292m); ground clearance 6.125in (15.6cm); turning circle 34ft (10.363m); kerb weight varies according to amount of fuel in tank, typically 16cwt 0qtr 16lb (820kg).
CAPACITIES: Fuel tank 8 gallons (36 litres). Boot 9.5ft^3 (0.269m^3).

Wolseley 1100 mark 2/1300

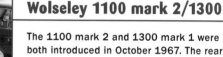

The 1100 mark 2 and 1300 mark 1 were both introduced in October 1967. The rear light arrangement and indicator repeater flashers on the front wings were revised, but the rear number plate lights remained unchanged. The styling of the car was done by the Italian company Pininfarina, who had also been responsible for the Austin

A40, and hints of A40 styling such as the short rear end can be seen in the 1100. The rear lights also have a similar outline on the earlier 1100 cars. The A40 was, however, a two-door car, and a version of it was available with an opening rear tailgate. Unlike its Austin/Morris counterparts, however, the Wolseley was never available in two-door or estate versions. The 1100 model was discontinued in October 1968.
Prices in 1967: 1100 – £801; 1300 manual – £825.
Price in 1968: automatic – £980.
Standard equipment included, walnut-veneered dashboard, glovebox with lid on passenger side, full width front parcel shelf and pockets in front doors, heater, windscreen washers, opening quarter lights in front doors, over-riders. Optional equipment included, radio, seat belts, auxiliary lights, full wheel trims, reclining front seats, Duotone colours, and, from October 1967, heated rear window and automatic transmission. Note some cars featured in this section have optional full wheel trims fitted in addition to the standard hub caps.

COLOURS: Single tone, Black, Snowberry White, Maroon, Damask Red, Glen Green, Connaught Green, Trafalgar Blue, Bermuda Blue, Farina Grey, Cumulus Grey, Fawn, Sandy Beige. Duotones, lower body and roof first: Trafalgar Blue/Black, Glen Green/Spruce Green, Farina Grey/Trafalgar Blue, Farina Grey/Maroon.

Above, manual gear change; right, automatic.

ENGINE (1100): Four-cylinder, OHV, bore 64.58mm, stroke 83.72mm, 1098cc (67.02in³), maximum bhp 55, two SU HS2 carburettors.
GEARBOX (1100): Four-speed, floor-mounted gear change, synchromesh on top three gears. Ratios: top 4.133, 3rd 5.83, 2nd 8.98, 1st 14.99.
ENGINE (1300): Four-cylinder, OHV, bore 70.61mm, stroke 81.28mm, 1275cc (77.82in³), maximum bhp 58, two SU HS4 carburettors, single with automatic transmission. SU HS2 all models from May 1968.

GEARBOX (1300): Four-speed, floor-mounted gear change, synchromesh on all gears. Ratios: top 3.65, 3rd 5.323, 2nd 8.10, 1st 12.89; with optional automatic gearbox, top 3.76, 3rd 5.49, 2nd 6.96, 1st 10.12.
BRAKES: Lockheed, with pressure-limiting valve fitted to more accurately apportion braking between front and rear wheels, front 8in discs and rear 8in drums.
STEERING: Rack and pinion.
TYRES: 5.50 x 12.
SUSPENSION: Front independent wishbone, rear independent trailing arms and anti-roll bar, front and rear interconnected Hydrolastic displacers.
DIMENSIONS: Length 12ft 2.75in (9.39m); width 5ft 0.4in (1.534m); height 4ft 4.7in (1.34m); wheelbase 7ft 9.5in (2.375m); track front 4ft 3.5in (1.308m); rear 4ft 2.9in (1.292m); ground clearance 6.125in (15.6cm); turning circle 34ft (10.363m); kerb weight, varies according to model, typically 16cwt 0qtr 16lb (820kg) to 16cwt 2qtr 4lb (840kg).
CAPACITIES: Fuel tank 8 gallons (36 litres). Boot 9.5ft³ (0.269m³).

Wolseley 1300 mark 2

In October 1968, the 1100 model was discontinued, and the 1300 became the mark 2. Improvements included larger front disc brakes, rocker switches instead of the toggle type that protruded from the dashboard, front seats which could now be tilted forward, allowing a more upright driving position, and variable distance from the steering wheel. A folding centre armrest was fitted for the rear seat, and armrests for the front doors; the front door bins were replaced with an expanding fabric pocket, and the option of Duotone paint scheme was lost. Also new was a combined boot handle and number plate light, replacing the separate boot lock and the two number plate lights fitted to earlier models. The front of the car remained unchanged with its traditional grille, whereas the equivalent Austin and Morris models received regular styling changes to the front grille.

Standard equipment included, walnut-veneered dashboard, glovebox with lid on passenger side, full width front parcel shelf and pockets in front doors, heater, windscreen washers, opening quarter lights in front doors, over-riders, and more. Optional factory fitted equipment in 1969 included, reclining front seats £15.19s.5d (£15.99), heated rear window £15.19s.5d (£15.99) and automatic

| TEMP | SPEEDO | FUEL |

Instrument layout.

45

transmission £95.16s.8d (£95.83). Dealer fitted items such as radio and seat belts incurred a separate fitting charge in addition to the price of the item. Prices of accessories from an independent supplier for owners to fit themselves, wheel trims £2.15s (£2.75), fog and spot lights with cable and switch £3.19s.6d (£3.97) each, reversing light kit for fitting below the bumper £2.8s (£2.40), rear window anti-condensation panel £0.14s.6d (£0.73). For comparison with the above, the 1969 price of a Wolseley 1300 was £883.75

bar, front and rear interconnected Hydrolastic displacers.

DIMENSIONS: Length 12ft 2.75in (9.39m); width 5ft 0.4in (1.534m); height 4ft 4.7in (1.34m); wheelbase 7ft 9.5in (2.375m); track front 4ft 3.5in (1.308m); rear 4ft 2.9in (1.292m); ground clearance 6.125in (15.6cm); turning circle 34ft (10.363m); kerb weight varies according to model, typically 16cwt 0qtr 16lb (820kg) to 16cwt 2qtr 4lb (840kg).

CAPACITIES: Fuel tank 8 gallons (36 litres). Boot 9.5ft^3 (0.269m^3).

ENGINE: Four-cylinder, OHV, bore 70.61mm, stroke 81.28mm, 1275cc (77.82in^3), maximum bhp 58, two SU HS2 carburettors, single SU HS4 with automatic transmission.

GEARBOX: Four-speed, floor-mounted gear change, synchromesh on all gears. Ratios: top 3.65, 3rd 5.323, 2nd 8.10, 1st 12.89; with optional automatic gearbox, top 3.76, 3rd 5.49, 2nd 6.96, 1st 10.12. Front-wheel drive with helical spur gears and open drive shafts with universal joints.

BRAKES: Lockheed, with pressure-limiting valve fitted to more accurately apportion braking between front and rear wheels, front 8.39in discs and rear 8in drums. Note increase in front wheel disc size, mark 1 was 8in.

STEERING: Rack and pinion.

TYRES: 5.50 x 12.

SUSPENSION: Front independent wishbone, rear independent trailing arms and anti-roll

Wolseley 1300 mark 3

Introduced in September 1971, the only noticeable difference from the mark 2 was the loss of the indicator repeater flashers from the front wings. The electrical system was changed to negative earth. The 1300 was discontinued in 1973 only two years after the rear-wheel drive 16/60 that had been introduced six years before it.

Total numbers produced 1965-1973: 1100 approximately 17,000; 1300 approximately 27,000.

Price when introduced in 1971: £993.

Price when discontinued in 1973: £1077.

Standard equipment included, walnut-veneered dashboard, glovebox with lid on passenger side, full width front parcel shelf and pockets in front doors, heater, windscreen washers, opening quarter lights in front doors, over-riders.

COLOURS: Now generally as other BMC 1300 models, all single tone, Flame Red, Mallard Green, Racing Green, Teal Blue, Midnight Blue, Blue Royale, Harvest Gold, Antelope, Limeflower, Wild Moss.

ENGINE: Four-cylinder, OHV, bore 70.61 mm, stroke 81.28 mm, 1275cc (77.82in^3), maximum bhp 58, two SU HS2 carburettors, single SU HS4 with automatic transmission.

47

GEARBOX: Four-speed, floor-mounted gear change, synchromesh on all gears. Ratios: top 3.65, 3rd 5.323, 2nd 8.10, 1st 12.89. Front-wheel drive with helical spur gears and open drive shafts with universal joints.

BRAKES: Lockheed, with pressure-limiting valve fitted to more accurately apportion braking between front and rear wheels and reduce risk of skidding when braking, front 8.39in discs and rear 8in drums.

STEERING: Rack and pinion.

TYRES: 5.50 x 12, spare wheel in a covered recess under the boot floor.

SUSPENSION: Front independent wishbone, rear independent trailing arms and anti-roll bar, front and rear interconnected Hydrolastic displacers.

DIMENSIONS: Length 12ft 2.75in (9.39m); width 5ft 0.4in (1.534m); height 4ft 4.7in (1.34m); wheelbase 7ft 9.5in (2.375m); track front 4ft 3.5in (1.308m); rear 4ft 2.9in (1.292m); ground clearance 6.125in (15.6cm); turning circle 34ft (10.363m); kerb weight varies according to model typically 16cwt 0qtr 16lb (820kg) to 16cwt 2qtr 4lb (840kg).

CAPACITIES: Fuel tank 8 gallons (36 litres). Boot 9.5ft³ (0.269m³).

Gear change diagram.

Instrument layout.

Wolseley 15/60

Introduced in 1958, this was the first of the medium-sized Farina family of cars to be launched. Unlike its Austin and Morris counterparts, however, there was never an estate variant. The Farina name is derived from the Pininfarina styling house in Italy that was responsible for the cars' design. Although the 15/60 is often thought of as the first of the Farina range to be launched, it was actually the smaller Austin A40 that was the first Pininfarina car to appear, albeit only a few months earlier. The 15/60 is easily identified from the 16/60 by its pointed tail fins: a popular styling feature of 1950s cars. However, the equivalent MG and Riley models had the less pronounced shorter tail fins from the start. A point of note is that, whilst the Wolseley cars had a Duotone paint scheme, with the roof and lower half painted the same colour, and a contrasting coloured middle section, the other Farina cars had the roof, top half of the rear wings and boot lid painted in one colour, and the bonnet and lower half of the car in another.

Number produced: 24,579.
Price when introduced: £991.
The standard equipment included water temperature and oil pressure gauges,

clock, heater, lockable glovebox, divided front bench seat with individual adjustment mechanism for each half, windscreen washers, reversing lights, over-riders and more. Optional equipment included radio, wheel rim embellishers, Duotone paintwork.

COLOURS (1960): Maroon, Smoke Grey, Old English White, Whitehall Beige, Black. Duotones, roof and lower body colour first: Maroon/Whitehall Beige, Smoke Grey/Navy Blue, Yukon Grey/Old English White, Porcelain Green/Connaught Green.

ENGINE: Four-cylinder, OHV, bore 73.025mm, stroke 88.9mm, 1489cc (90.88in³), maximum bhp 55, single SU HS2 carburettor.

GEARBOX: Four-speed, floor-mounted gear change, synchromesh on top three gears. Ratios: top 4.55, 3rd 6.25, 2nd 10.08, 1st 16.55.

REAR AXLE: Hypoid bevel, three quarter floating.

Instrument layout.

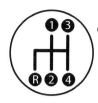

Gear change diagram.

BRAKES: Girling, front and rear 9in drums, handbrake between driver's seat and door.
STEERING: Cam and peg.
TYRES: 5.90 x 14, spare wheel in tray underneath the rear of the car, lowered by unscrewing a bolt located in a readily accessible position inside the boot.
SUSPENSION: Front, coil spring and wishbone, rear semi-elliptic leaf springs, telescopic shock absorbers front and rear.
DIMENSIONS: Length 14ft 10.5in (4.534m); width 5ft 3.5in (1.613m); height 4ft 11.75in

The rear boot lid of all models had a separate section near the rear screen for the lockable fuel filler flap. Care was required when filling up not to spill fuel over the top of the rear wing.

51

(1.518m); wheelbase 8ft 3.25in (2.521m); track front 4ft 0.875in (1.241m); rear 4ft 1.875in (1.267m); ground clearance 6.25in (15.9cm); turning circle 37ft 6in (11.43m); weight 1ton 2cwt 0qtr 9lb (1120kg). **CAPACITIES:** Fuel 10 gallons (45 litres). Boot 19ft^3 (0.538m^3).

Left, 15/60; right, 16/60.

Note different style of rear wing and lights, and also that over-riders are part of the rear light arrangement on the 16/60.

Wolseley 16/60

Introduced in 1961, this was a restyled and upgraded 15/60, with a larger engine. It had an unusually long life, and was eventually discontinued in early 1971 at the same time as the Morris Oxford (of the other Farina cars, the MG Magnette had been discontinued in 1968, and the Austin Cambridge and Riley 4/72 models in 1969). The 16/60 can be easily distinguished from the 15/60 by its different tail fins. Other styling changes included extending the side trim forward to the headlights, moving the front and rear over-riders outwards, with the rear over-riders now forming part of the lower rear light arrangement (which had the effect of reducing the overall length of the car). Improvements over the 15/60 included an enlarged engine of 1622cc, a longer wheelbase achieved by moving the rear axle backwards, a wider front and rear track, and the fitment of front and rear anti-roll bars. Further improvements occurred at various stages throughout its life, including the elimination of some greasing points.
Number produced: 63,082.
Price when introduced: £993.

Instrument layout.

52

Gear change diagram.

A version of the 16/60 with a six-cylinder 2433cc (148.5in³) engine, called the 24/80, was produced in Australia. It was launched in 1962, initially using the rear wing style of the 15/60, but had the lengthened wheelbase of the 16/60 body from the start. An Austin version was also built, known as the Freeway, and available as both a saloon and an estate, but lack of sales led to them being discontinued in 1965. The blue car featured in this section (registration number EOL 683C) is an Australian 24/80, dimensions as follows: length 14ft 10in (4.521m), width 5ft 3.5in (1.613m), height 4ft 10in (1.473m).

Standard equipment for the 16/60 at the start included water temperature and oil pressure gauges, clock, heater, lockable glovebox, divided front bench seat with individual adjustment for each half, reversing lights, over-riders, and more. Optional extras included radio, automatic transmission, wheel rim embellishers, Duotone paintwork, laminated windscreen, seatbelts, and more. Later cars also had the option of reclining front seats and heated rear window, but, by 1969, the option of Duotone paintwork was gone. October 1966 optional extra prices, automatic transmission £83.87, reclining

front seats £15.37. (Prices include Purchase
Tax). For comparison purposes a saloon
cost £868.28 in 1966 (Purchase Tax rates
had decreased since the car was launched,
hence the price was lower than in 1961.)

COLOURS (1962): Maroon, Rose Taupe,
Dove Grey, Porcelain Green, Ice Blue, Black.
Duotones, roof and lower body colour first:
Maroon/Dove Grey, Dove Grey/Old English
White, Rose Taupe/Sandy Beige, Ice Blue/
Old English White.
ENGINE (1962 specification): Four-cylinder,
OHV, bore 76.2mm, stroke 88.9mm, 1622cc
(98.94in^3), maximum bhp 61, single SU HS2
carburettor.

GEARBOX: Four-speed, floor-mounted gear
change, automatic optional, synchromesh on
top three gears. Ratios: top 4.3, 3rd 5.91,
2nd 9.52, 1st 15.64.
REAR AXLE: Hypoid bevel, three quarter
floating. Ratio early cars 4.55:1, later cars
4.3:1.
BRAKES: Girling, front and rear 9in drums,
handbrake between driver's seat and door.
STEERING: Cam and peg.
TYRES: 5.90 x 14, spare wheel in tray
underneath the rear of the car.
SUSPENSION: Front, coil spring and
wishbone, rear semi-elliptic leaf springs,
telescopic shock absorbers and anti-roll bars
front and rear.
DIMENSIONS: Length 14ft 6.5in (4.432m);

width 5ft 3.5in (1.613m); height 4ft 10.875in (1.495m); wheelbase 8ft 4.25in (2.546m); track front 4ft 2.625in (1.286m); rear 4ft 3.375in (1.305m); ground clearance 6.5in (16.51cm); turning circle 37ft (11.278m); weight 1ton 2cwt 0qtr 11lb (1122kg).

CAPACITIES: Fuel 10 gallons (45 litres). Boot 19ft^3 (0.538m^3).

Wolseley 6/99

Introduced in 1959 to replace the 6/90, this Farina-designed car was based on the Austin A99, but had extra equipment and better trim. Previous Wolseleys had been part of the Nuffield organisation, and had shared components with the Morris and Riley cars, but the new 6/99 was now part of the BMC range. In general appearance, it looked like the 15/60 of 1958. The 6/99, in its 6/110 guise, would be discontinued in 1968, whereas the 16/60 (the later version of the 15/60) would continue until 1971. The Wolseley 15/60 had been introduced before its Austin counterpart, the Cambridge, but the Austin A99 Westminster was launched before the Wolseley 6/99. There was also a third variant, the Vanden Plas Princess 3-litre, which was placed above the Wolseley 6/99 in the BMC range; the Vanden Plas cars had originally been large upmarket Austin cars prior to the creation of BMC. The engine in the 6/99 was first used in the Wolseley 6/90 as a 2639cc unit, then the Austin-Healey 100-Six, as well as the Austin-Healey 3000 sports car. The gear change for the 6/99 reverted to the column change used on the early model 6/90 cars, but overdrive was now standard.

All models had a separate section on the boot lid for the lockable fuel filler flap.

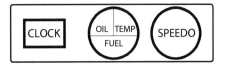

Instrument layout.

stroke 88.9mm, 2912cc (177.63in³),
maximum bhp 103, two SU H4 carburettors.
GEARBOX: Three speed, steering column
gear change, Borg-Warner overdrive standard
on top and 2nd, all synchromesh gearbox.
Ratios: o/d top 2.74, top 3.91, o/d 2nd
4.52, 2nd 6.45, 1st 12.10; with optional
automatic: top 3.55, 2nd 5.09, 1st 8.19.
REAR AXLE: Hypoid bevel, three quarter
floating.
BRAKES: Lockheed, power assisted, front
10.75in discs, rear 10in drums, handbrake
between driver's seat and door.
STEERING: Cam and lever.
TYRES: 7.00 x 14, spare wheel in tray
underneath the rear of the car, lowered
by unscrewing a bolt located in a readily
accessible position inside the boot.
SUSPENSION: Front, wishbones and coil
springs, rear semi-elliptic leaf springs, lever
type shock absorbers and anti-roll bars front
and rear.
DIMENSIONS: Length 15ft 8in (4.775m);
width 5ft 8.5in (1.74m); height 4ft 11in
(1.499m); wheelbase 9ft (2.743m); track
front 4ft 6in (1.372m); rear 4ft 5.25in
(1.352m); ground clearance 6.375in
(16.19cm); turning circle 40ft (12.192m);
kerb weight 1ton 10cwt 2qtr (1549kg).
CAPACITIES: Fuel 16 gallons (73 litres).
Boot 18ft³ (0.51m³).

Number produced: 13,108.
Price when introduced: £1254.
Standard equipment included water
temperature and oil pressure gauges, clock,
two speed wipers, twin long range driving
lights. Optional equipment included radio,
automatic transmission.
ENGINE: Six-cylinder, OHV, bore 83.34mm,

57

Wolseley 6/110 mark 1

Introduced in 1961 to replace the 6/99, changes included a longer wheelbase, achieved by moving the rear axle further back to minimise wheelarch intrusion into the interior, and a floor-mounted gear change. This, however, now made it difficult to seat three in the front, even though the bench seat, as used in the 6/99, had been retained. An ammeter was now standard equipment, and was incorporated in the same instrument dial as the fuel, temperature and oil pressure gauges, thereby avoiding the need to reorganise the dashboard layout. Externally, only the new 6/110 badges on the rear distinguished it from the 6/99. There were no changes to the rear lights or tail fins as there had been with the 15/60 and 16/60 models. The spare wheel remained under the boot floor in a separate carrier that could be lowered without moving any luggage, and it also meant that there was no need to put a wet or muddy wheel into the boot in the event of a puncture. The handbrake was by the right-hand side of the driver's seat: a feature still used by several car manufacturers during the 1960s, whilst some had the handbrake underneath the dashboard, such as in the Wolseley 6/90 and 18/85. It was not until the 1970s that a handbrake placed centrally between the front seats became universally adopted.

Gear change diagram.

Green, Rose Taupe, Mist Grey, Trafalgar Blue, Black. Duotones, lower body and roof first: Arianca Beige/Sandy Beige, Porcelain Green/Connaught Green, Rose Taupe/Sandy Beige, Trafalgar Blue/Mist Grey.

ENGINE: Six-cylinder, OHV, bore 83.34mm, stroke 88.9mm, 2912cc (177.63in^3), maximum bhp 120, two SU H4 carburettors.

GEARBOX: Three speed all synchromesh gearbox, floor-mounted gear change, Borg-Warner overdrive standard on top and second. Ratios: o/d top 2.74, top 3.91, o/d 2nd 4.95, 2nd 6.45, 1st 12.10, with optional automatic. Ratios: top 3.55, 2nd 5.15, 3rd 8.48

REAR AXLE: Hypoid bevel, three quarter floating. Ratio: manual 3.9, automatic 3.55.

BRAKES: Lockheed, power assisted front 10in discs, rear 10in drums.

STEERING: Cam and lever.

TYRES: 7.00 x 14, spare wheel in tray underneath the rear of the car.

SUSPENSION: Front, wishbones and coil springs, rear semi-elliptic leaf springs, lever type shock absorbers and anti-roll bars front and rear.

DIMENSIONS: Length 15ft 8in (4.775m); width 5ft 8.5in (1.74m); height 5ft 0in (1.524m); wheelbase 9ft 2in (2.79m); track front 4ft 5.8125in (1.366m); rear 4ft 5.25in (1.352m); ground clearance 6.25in (15.875cm); turning circle 41ft (12.5m); weight 1ton 11cwt (1575kg).

CAPACITIES: Fuel 16 gallons (73 litres). Boot 18ft^3 (0.51m^3).

Number produced: 10,800.
Price when introduced: £1343.
Standard equipment included water temperature and oil pressure gauges, ammeter, clock, two speed wipers, windscreen washers, opening quarter lights on all doors, map pockets in front doors, leather upholstery with divided front bench seat, twin long range driving lights, reversing light and more. Optional equipment included radio, automatic transmission and Duotone paint scheme.

COLOURS (1961): Arianca Beige, Porcelain

Wolseley 6/110 mark 2

The mark 2, introduced in 1964, featured reclining front seats and a four-speed gearbox, but overdrive became an optional extra. Other changes included smaller wheels, now 13in instead of 14in, increased length rear leaf springs with twin telescopic shock absorbers, and no anti-roll bar. The front suspension received new type shock absorbers, but retained the anti-roll bar. Greasing points were now eliminated from the steering column, the dashboard was revised with the clock now in front of the driver, the front seats were raised, and map pockets were added to the rear doors. The 6/110 mark 2 was discontinued in March 1968, however, unlike its Austin counterpart, the Westminster A110 (which was also discontinued in early 1968), there was no replacement. A new Austin model, the 3-litre, which resembled a large 1800 'Land crab,' but which had traditional rear-wheel drive, was introduced at the 1967 Motor Show. Plans for Wolseley and Vanden Plas models were considered, but with BMC having acquired Jaguar, and the merger with British Leyland, manufacturers of Rover and Triumph, imminent, it seemed there were already enough models to fill the luxury end of the market.

Instrument layout.

Number produced: 13,301.
Price when introduced: £1180 (a Wolseley
Hornet cost £557 at this time).
Standard equipment included water
temperature and oil pressure gauges,
ammeter, clock, two speed wipers,
windscreen washers, leather upholstery,
individual reclining front seats with folding
picnic tables in the back of them for use
by rear seat passengers, map pockets in

all doors, twin long range driving lights, reversing light and more. Optional equipment included radio, overdrive, Borg-Warner 35 automatic transmission, Hydrosteer power assisted steering, Normalair air-conditioning and Duotone paint scheme. October 1966 optional extra prices: overdrive £52.24, automatic transmission £98.33, power-assisted steering £67.60 (prices include Purchase Tax). For comparison purposes, a saloon cost £1200 in 1966.

COLOURS: Porcelain Green, Rose Taupe, Trafalgar Blue, Black. Duotones, lower body and roof first: Porcelain Green/Connaught Green, and more, with a variety of colours similar to the mark 1.

ENGINE: Six-cylinder, OHV, bore 83.34mm, stroke 88.9mm, 2912cc (177.63in³), maximum bhp 120, two SU H4 carburettors.

GEARBOX: Four-speed, floor-mounted gear change, overdrive optional, synchromesh on top three gears. Ratios: top 3.91, 3rd 5.11, 2nd 8.10, 1st 10.31; with optional automatic: top 3.55, 2nd 5.15, 3rd 8.48.

REAR AXLE: Hypoid bevel, three quarter floating.

BRAKES: Lockheed, power assisted with pressure-limiting valve fitted to more accurately apportion braking between front and rear wheels to reduce risk of skidding

Left, manual gear change; right, automatic gear change.

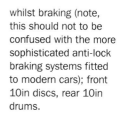

Car above has a fabric sunroof.

whilst braking (note, this should not to be confused with the more sophisticated anti-lock braking systems fitted to modern cars); front 10in discs, rear 10in drums.
STEERING: Cam and lever, power assistance optional.
TYRES: 7.50 x 13.
SUSPENSION: Front, coil springs, telescopic shock absorbers and anti-roll bar, rear semi-elliptic leaf springs and twin telescopic shock absorbers.

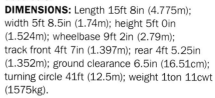

DIMENSIONS: Length 15ft 8in (4.775m); width 5ft 8.5in (1.74m); height 5ft 0in (1.524m); wheelbase 9ft 2in (2.79m); track front 4ft 7in (1.397m); rear 4ft 5.25in (1.352m); ground clearance 6.5in (16.51cm); turning circle 41ft (12.5m); weight 1ton 11cwt (1575kg).
CAPACITIES: Fuel 16 gallons (73 litres). Boot 18ft^3 (0.51m^3).

Wolseley 18/85 mark 1

This was the Wolseley equivalent of the Austin and Morris 1800, albeit introduced two and a half years later in 1967, and was the last of the family of front-wheel drive cars to be associated with Alec Issigonis. It was readily recognisable from its lesser siblings by its Wolseley front grille with traditional illuminated badge, and a unique rear light arrangement. In true Wolseley style, it had walnut-trimmed dashboard and door cappings, and leather seats. It did not, however, have opening quarter lights in the front doors – instead it had vents at the ends of the dashboard to provide fresh air, which could be directed towards occupants or the front door window glass to aid demisting. Opening rear quarter lights behind the rear doors aided the flow of air through the car. It was the last in this particular range of cars to be produced, as there were never any MG or Riley versions of the 1800 to follow the 18/85 (whereas in the 1100/1300 range, the Austin, Morris and MG versions had been followed by Wolseley and Riley variants). Anyone desiring one of these marques had to choose between the front-wheel drive 1300 range, or the rear-wheel drive Magnette and 4/72. This was the start of rationalisation of BMC models, and by 1970 there were

no more Riley cars; the only remaining traditional rear-wheel drive cars were the Wolseley 16/60 and Morris Minor. A rear-wheel drive version of the 1800, the Austin 3-Litre (introduced to replace both the Austin A110 and Wolseley 6/110) was only built for three years until early 1971. There was never a Wolseley rear-wheel drive version of this car. The introduction of the 18/85 also saw the end of the general association between Wolseley cars and police forces around the country.

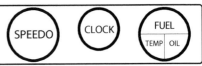

Instrument layout.

Number produced: 18/85, mark 1 and 2 – 35,597.

Price when introduced: £1040.

Standard equipment included water temperature and oil pressure gauges, clock, heater, walnut-trimmed fascia and door cappings, lockable glovebox, anti-glare interior mirror, opening rear quarter lights, front and rear door pockets with scuff plates, door sill tread plates, reversing light, over-riders with rubber inserts, side repeater indicators on the front wings, lockable fuel filler flap, wheel hub caps with 'W' motif. Optional extras included radio, reclining front seats (standard on mark 2 models), seat belts, automatic transmission, heated rear window.

COLOURS: The BMC range of colours

Left, manual gear change (floor-mounted); right, automatic gear change diagram, dashboard mounted.

Rear lights: left, Wolseley 18/85 mark 1 and 2; middle, Austin/Morris mark 1; right, Austin/Morris mark 2.

applied to cars of the period included Antelope, Maroon, Black, Glacier White, Everglade, Damask Red, Harvest Gold, Teal Blue.

ENGINE: Four-cylinder, OHV, bore 80.26mm, stroke 88.9mm, 1798cc (109.67in³), maximum bhp 86, single SU HS6 carburettor.

GEARBOX: Four-speed, floor-mounted gear change, three-speed automatic optional, all synchromesh gearbox. Ratios: top 3.88, 3rd 5.37, 2nd 7.99, 1st 12.78. Front-wheel drive with helical spur gears and open drive shafts with universal joints.

BRAKES: Power assisted with pressure limiting valve fitted to more accurately apportion braking between front and rear wheels, this should not to be confused with the more sophisticated anti-lock braking systems that started to appear on cars during the mid-1980s. Front 9.28in discs, rear 9in drums.

STEERING: Power assisted rack and pinion.

TYRES: 175 x 13, spare wheel in tray under boot floor as 16/60 model, lowered by unscrewing a bolt.

SUSPENSION: Front independent with upper and lower arms and tie rods, swivel axles mounted on ball joints, rear independent with trailing arms, front and rear with interconnected Hydrolastic displacers.

DIMENSIONS: Length 13ft 10.1in (4.219m); width 5ft 7in (1.702 m); height 4ft 7.5in (1.410m); wheelbase 8ft 10in (2.69m); track front 4ft 8.5in (1.435m); rear 4ft 7.5in (1.41m); ground clearance 6.625in (16.83cm); turning circle 38ft 6in (11.735m); weight 1ton 2cwt 3qtr (1155.7kg).

CAPACITIES: Fuel 10.5 gallons (48 litres). Boot 17.0ft³ (0.48m³).

Wolseley 18/85 mark 2

The mark 2 was introduced in August
1969 to replace the mark 1 model. The
only external difference was the addition
of a small badge on the rear boot lid
denoting this was a mark 2, for, unlike its
Austin and Morris counterparts, the rear
light arrangement and front grille did not
change when the mark 2 model appeared.
The change from 13in to 14in wheels was
probably less apparent. Other changes
included a revised interior, with reclining
front seats as standard, but the useful
front and rear door bins were replaced by
elasticated pockets on the front doors and
backs of the front seats; seat surfaces were
now vinyl, not leather. New flush-fitting
interior door handles and modified window
winder handles, together with a new lever
on the steering column that controlled
headlight high/low beam, headlight flasher,
horn and indicators, created a more modern
looking interior. Personally, I preferred the
original horn button in the middle of the
steering wheel, as found on the mark 1,
but having inadvertently damaged a few
floor-mounted dip switches, by kicking them
in my haste to dim the lights, I welcomed
the move to the steering column type.
The introduction of two-speed wipers, and

This red car on this page is an S model.

moving the heater controls and dashboard mounted handbrake nearer to the driver were also useful improvements, but it was not until the introduction of the Wolseley Six in 1972 that the handbrake would eventually move to the floor between the front seats. Also introduced with the mark 2 was an additional model: a more powerful S version with twin SU carburettors, which can be identified by its 'S' badge on the rear boot lid and moulded side trim strip. Standard equipment for both included water temperature and oil pressure gauges, clock, heater, walnut-trimmed fascia and door cappings, lockable glovebox, parcel shelves either side of centre console, anti-glare interior mirror, reclining front seats, opening rear quarter lights, front door map pockets, door sill tread plates, two-speed wipers and electrically operated windscreen washers, reversing light, over-riders with rubber inserts, side repeater indicators on the front wings, lockable fuel filler flap, wheel hub caps with 'W' motif. Optional extras included radio, seat belts, automatic transmission, heated rear window.

ENGINE: Four-cylinder, OHV, bore 80.26mm, stroke 88.9mm, 1798cc (109.67in^3), maximum bhp 86, single SU HS6 carburettor, S model maximum bhp 95.5, twin SU HS6 carburettors.
GEARBOX: Four-speed, floor-mounted gear change, three-speed automatic optional, all synchromesh gearbox. Ratios: top 3.88, 3rd 5.37, 2nd 7.99, 1st 12.78. Front-wheel drive with helical spur gears and open drive shafts with universal joints.
BRAKES: Power assisted with pressure limiting valve fitted to more accurately apportion braking between front and rear wheels, front 9.28in discs, rear 9in drums, S model front 9.7 in discs, rear 9in drums.
STEERING: Power assisted rack and pinion.
TYRES: 165 x 14.
SUSPENSION: Front independent with upper and lower arms and tie rods, swivel axles mounted on ball joints, rear independent with trailing arms, front and rear with interconnected Hydrolastic displacers.
DIMENSIONS: Length 13ft 11in (4.24m); width 5ft 7in (1.702m); height 4ft 7.5in

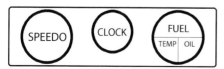

Instrument layout.

69

(1.410m); wheelbase 8ft 10in (2.69m); track front 4ft 8.5in (1.435m); rear 4ft 7.5in (1.41m); ground clearance 6.625in (16.83cm); turning circle 38ft 6in (11.735m); weight 1ton 2cwt 3qtr (1155.7kg).
CAPACITIES: Fuel 10.5 gallons (48 litres). Boot 17.0ft³ (0.48m³).

Wolseley Six

Introduced in March 1972, this was essentially a Wolseley 18/85 with an entirely new six-cylinder engine. This engine, which was subsequently carried over to the 18/22, had been derived from the Austin Maxi four-cylinder engine, rather than being an 18/85 engine with two extra cylinders. This new engine was called the E-series, the six-cylinder 6/110 engine, the C-series, was too long to be installed transversely, unlike the B-series engine from the 16/60 which had been successfully turned around and fitted into the 18/85. BMC had earlier been able to use the A-series engine from the Austin A35, and mount that transversely into the Hornet, and the experience learned when fitting the gearbox underneath the engine with the A-series enabled a similar arrangement to be adopted for the B-series engine when it was fitted into the 18/85. Although Austin and Morris continued to produce the original four-cylinder 1800 alongside their new six-cylinder 2200 model, both versions of the 18/85 were dropped from the Wolseley range, leaving the Six to effectively replace the 18/85 S. The extra length of the six-cylinder engine meant that the radiator could not be fitted against the inner wheelarch, as had been the case with other transversely-mounted engines, so it had to be fitted at the front of the engine compartment in a more traditional manner. This had the advantage that it kept water from being blown through the front grille, so a plastic cover was no longer needed to keep the electrical components dry. It did, however, mean that an electric fan had to be fitted, as it could no longer be driven by a belt at the front of the engine. Also at this time, an alternator replaced the dynamo, a larger fuel tank was fitted, and the handbrake was moved from beneath the dashboard to a new location between the front seats, but power steering was now an optional extra. A Six badge on the boot lid replaced the 18/85 numbers, and the over-riders and S model side trim were removed. **Number produced:** 25,214.
Price in August 1972: (a few months after it was launched) £1606; but by January

1975, when it was discontinued, the price had risen to £2327.
Standard equipment included water temperature and oil pressure gauges, clock, heater, individual reclining front seats with foldaway armrests, front and rear seats trimmed in velour style brushed nylon, two-speed windscreen wipers, electric windscreen washers, steering column lock and more. Optional extras included automatic transmission, heated rear window, power-assisted steering, Rostyle wheels.

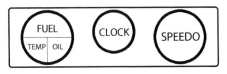

Instrument layout.

COLOURS: included Limeflower, Racing Green, Old English White and more.
ENGINE: Six-cylinder, OHC, bore 76.2mm, stroke 81.28mm, 2227cc (135.8in^3), maximum bhp 110, twin SU HS6 carburettors early cars, twin SU HIF6 carburettors later cars.
GEARBOX: Four-speed, floor-mounted gear change, now rod rather than cable operated, three-speed automatic optional, all synchromesh gearbox. Ratios: top 3.88, 3rd 5.37, 2nd 7.99, 1st 12.78. Front-wheel drive with open drive shafts with universal joints.
BRAKES: Girling, power assisted with pressure limiting valve fitted to more accurately apportion braking between front and rear wheels, thus reducing the likelihood of skidding

Manual gear change diagram.

when braking, front 9.7in discs, rear 9in drums.
STEERING: Cam Gears, rack and pinion, power assistance optional.
TYRES: 165 x 14.
SUSPENSION: Front independent with wishbones, rear independent with trailing arms, front and rear with inter-connected Hydrolastic displacers.
DIMENSIONS: Length 13ft 10.5in (4.23m); width 5ft 7in (1.7m); height 4ft 8in (1.43m); wheelbase 8ft 10in (2.69m); track front 4ft 8.5in (1.435m); rear 4ft 7.5in (1.41m); ground clearance 6.625in (17cm); turning circle 38ft 6in (11.7m); weight 1ton 3cwt 1qtr 13lb (1187kg).
CAPACITIES: Fuel tank 12.5 gallons (56.8 litres). Boot 17.0ft^3 (0.48m^3).

Wolseley 18/22

Introduced in March 1975 to replace the Wolseley Six, this was an entirely new design by Harris Mann, who had also been responsible for designing the Austin Allegro and Triumph TR7. Initially there were Wolseley, Austin and Morris variants of the 18/22, the Wolseley model referred to in brochures as the Wolseley Saloon had its own unique frontal treatment, a full vinyl roof, full width rubber inserts in the bumpers and special wheel trims, it was also better equipped internally with plush velour cloth trim, wood inlaid fascia, tinted glass and a fully carpeted boot with light. The Hydrolastic suspension used in earlier front-wheel drive Wolseleys was replaced by Hydragas suspension – another idea developed by Alex Moulton, and which had originally been introduced with the Austin Allegro. To describe it in its simplest form, this new system used pressurised nitrogen units instead of rubber cones within the interconnected front and rear suspension. Wider section tyres of same diameter, the reintroduction of power steering as standard, together with the addition of a host of equipment that had previously been on the optional extras list, were improvements over the Six. With the proliferation of cars now wearing Austin, Morris and Wolseley badges – there were 1800, 1800 HL, and 2200 HL

Austin and Morris models – the decision was ultimately made to simplify the range, and the car was renamed as the Princess with four models – the 1800, 1800 HL, 2200 HL and 2200 HLS – instead of the original seven. Thus, by September 1975, there were no more cars carrying the Wolseley name. **Number produced: 3800.**
Standard equipment included temperature gauge, voltmeter, clock, warning lights for low oil pressure, brake line failure and more,

radio and fully retractable aerial, heater with three-speed fan, reclining front seats, driver's seat height adjustable, dipping rear view mirror, vanity mirror on passengers sunvisor, front seat belts, heated rear window, two-speed wipers with flick-wipe and electric windscreen washers controlled by a single lever on the left-hand side of the steering column, combined ignition switch and steering column lock, interior bonnet release, door sill tread plates, twin exterior door mirrors, reversing lights, hazard warning lights, locking petrol filler cap, vinyl covered roof. Optional extras included automatic transmission, head restraints, rear seat belts, Denovo run flat wheels and tyres, laminated windscreen, metallic paint finish.

ENGINE: Six-cylinder, OHC, bore 76.2mm, stroke 81.28mm, 2227cc (135.8in³), maximum bhp 110, twin SU HIF6 carburettors.

GEARBOX: Four-speed, floor-mounted gear change, three-speed automatic optional, all synchromesh gearbox. Ratios: top 3.72, 3rd 5.13, 2nd 7.66, 1st 12.24, reverse 3.07:1. Front-wheel drive, open shafts with constant velocity joints, final drive ratio 3.72:1.

BRAKES: Power assisted, dual circuit, front 10.6in discs, rear 9in drums, handbrake between front seats.

STEERING: Power assisted rack and pinion.

TYRES: 185 x 14.

SUSPENSION: Front wishbone style upper and lower transverse arms, rear trailing arms with interconnected front and rear Hydragas units.

DIMENSIONS: Length 14ft 7.5in (4.455m); width 5ft 8in (1.727m); height 4ft 7.5in (1.409m); wheelbase 8ft 9.25in (2.673m); track front 4ft 10in (1.473m); rear 4ft 9.5in (1.457m); ground clearance 6.45in (16.4cm); turning circle 37ft 10in (11.53m); kerb weight 1ton 3cwt 3qtr 17lb (1215kg).

CAPACITIES: Fuel tank 16 gallons (72.7 litres). Boot 18.8ft³ (0.532m³).

Left, manual gear change diagram.
Below, instrument layout.

A history of the Riley Motor Company

William Riley, born in 1851, assumed responsibility of his family's weaving company in 1870. However, following the decline of the weaving industry after the Education Acts of the 1870s led to a reduction in the availability of cheap child labour, he turned his attention to other manufacturing businesses. In 1890 he acquired Bonnick and Company, whose cycle business led to the formation of the Riley Cycle Company. Like many bicycle manufacturers of the era, William soon turned his attention to the motor vehicle businesses that had sprung up around Coventry, and he and his sons built their first car in 1896.

There followed a period of experimenting with various engines and body styles before the brothers, led by Percy Riley (William's middle son out of five who all eventually became involved in the business), decided to concentrate on the manufacture of motor vehicles instead of bicycles. During that time they had set up a number of separate companies manufacturing car engines, wheels, bodies, etc, and the separate companies were later amalgamated to form Riley (Coventry) Ltd in the 1930s. In the meantime they had enjoyed motor racing success with a number of sporting models, generally based around the Riley Nine. They also adopted names that

would appear later on: the Kestrel and the Imp – a name subsequently used by the Rootes company for its small car.

Like many car manufacturers, however, financial difficulties led to the collapse of the company, at which point it was acquired in 1938 by William Morris and added to his Nuffield organisation, and Victor Riley, the oldest son, was given a role within the Riley element of the business. A new slogan 'Magnificent motoring' was introduced, however the original slogan 'As old as the industry, as modern as the hour' still sometimes appeared.

After the end of World War II in 1945, unlike many other motor manufactures that continued to build their prewar models for a few years, the Riley company introduced an entirely new range of cars, which subsequently became known as the RM models. These cars are regarded by many as being the last true Rileys. All future models were thought of as part of the BMC range, which saw the introduction of so-called badge engineering, where a universal bodyshell was utilised, fitted with engines of varying power and finished with differing interior trim.

The last Rileys were produced in 1969, following a reorganisation of the BMC model range to reduce the multitude of versions of a single car; as an example, there were over 20 variants of the 1100/1300 range around this time.

This car is an RM model that is outside the scope of the book.

Riley Pathfinder

The Riley Pathfinder was introduced in October 1953 to replace the RMF. It was sometimes referred to as the RMH model, however, its more familiar nickname was the 'Ditchfinder' because of problems associated with the Panhard rod which influenced the rear suspension's behaviour and, in some cases, led to loss of control of the vehicle. Other issues with the cars included varying pressure when operating the brakes, and water leaks. Although similar in appearance to the Wolseley Six-Ninety, the Pathfinder featured entirely different mechanical components, the most notable being that the Wolseley had a six-cylinder engine and the Riley a four-cylinder unit. However, the Pathfinder's replacement, the Riley Two-Point-Six, used the same engine as the Wolseley Six-Ninety series 3.

The Pathfinder continued the tradition of a separate chassis and body, with the body being produced by Fisher and Ludlow, a subsidiary of BMC. Gerald Palmer, who designed the Pathfinder, was also responsible for the design of other Nuffield/BMC cars, including the MG Magnette ZA. He had earlier worked for Jowett, where he had designed the Javelin – a car that was fitted with a 'flat-four' engine. Changes made during the Pathfinder's production life included the introduction of a completely new rear suspension, tyre sizes were changed, and dashboards redesigned. Standard equipment was impressive and included many items that were optional for a lot of other cars. For 1956 the standard equipment included: revolution counter, ammeter, oil pressure and water temperature gauges, heater, bench or bucket front seats trimmed in leather, armrests on passenger front and both rear doors, rear seat folding central armrest, polished wood dashboard and door trim, two sunvisors, glovebox with map reading light, two roof lights with separate controls, cigarette lighter, opening front quarter lights, windscreen washers, reversing lights, two front fog lights, trafficators or flashing indicators (according to country where vehicle was sold), and over-riders. Optional extras included a radio and, for later cars, overdrive.

Riley Two-Point-Six (2.6)

Number produced: 5536
Price when introduced: £1240

COLOURS: Black, Maroon, Cedar Green, Charcoal Grey, Kashmir Beige. Duotones, upper body first, Swiss Grey/Charcoal Grey, Blue/Steel Grey, Rose Taupe/Kashmir Beige.
ENGINE: Four-cylinder, OHV, bore 80.5mm, stroke 120mm, 2443cc (149.09in^3), maximum bhp 110 at 4400rpm, two SU HS4 carburettors.
GEARBOX: Four-speed, floor-mounted gear change between driver's seat and door, synchromesh on top three gears. Ratios: top 4.11, 3rd 5.88, 2nd 8.446, 1st 13.59, reverse 18.42, optional overdrive available from October 1955. Ratios: top 2.87, 3rd 4.11.
REAR AXLE: Early cars semi-floating, later cars three quarter floating, hypoid bevel. Ratio all cars: 4.11:1.
BRAKES: Girling, power assisted, front and rear 12in drums.
STEERING: Bishop cam and lever.
TYRES: Early cars 6.70 x 16, from 1955 to 1956, 6.00 x16, later cars 6.50 x 16.
SUSPENSION: Front, Riley independent with torsion bars and telescopic shock absorbers. Rear, initially coil springs, radius arms, Panhard rod (anti-roll bar) and telescopic shock absorbers; later cars semi-elliptic leaf springs and telescopic shock absorbers.
DIMENSIONS: Length 15ft 3in (4.65m); width 5ft 7in (1.70m); height 5ft 0in (1.52m); wheelbase 9ft 5.5in (2.88m); track front and rear 4ft 6.5in (1.38m); ground clearance 7in (18cm); turning circle 36ft (11m); weight approximately 1ton 10cwt (1524kg).
CAPACITIES: Fuel 13 gallons (59 litres). Boot 11ft^3 (0.3m^3).

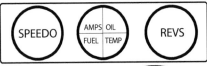

Instrument layout and gear change diagrams.

Introduced in 1957 to replace the Riley Pathfinder, and discontinued in September 1959, this was the last of the true Riley cars, with all future models being 'badge engineered' versions of other BMC models. The Two-Point-Six now adopted the BMC 'C' series six-cylinder engine, and was more closely aligned to its Wolseley Six-Ninety cousin. Changes from the Pathfinder, apart from the engine, included enlarging the rear window, flashing indicators were now standard, the front drum brakes were increased in size, but the gear change remained between the driver's seat and door (an uncommon feature), and the body and chassis were still of separate construction. This was the last of the large-engined Rileys, and saw a return to the practice of offering a two-model range – in this case the 4/Sixty Eight and One-Point-Five. With the introduction of these new models the standard practices such as mono-construction became the norm, and the handbrake was moved from under the dashboard to the side of the driver's seat on the 4/Sixty Eight and between the front seats on the One-Point-Five, with the gearlever in the centre of the car between the front seats on both models. Standard equipment included water temperature and oil pressure gauges, ammeter, clock, walnut facia and door cappings, heater, individual front bucket seats or divided front bench seat trimmed in leather, armrests on all doors, central folding armrest for rear seat, lockable glovebox, map reading light below facia, two sunvisors, two roof lights with separate controls, windscreen washers, opening front door quarter lights, fog and long range driving light, reversing light, over-riders, locking fuel filler flap, and more. Optional equipment included radio, overdrive or automatic transmission, and a Duotone paint finish.

COLOURS: Single tone, Black. Duotones, Leaf Green/Shannon Green, Teal Blue/Basilica Blue, Frilford Grey/Charcoal Grey, Kashmir Beige/Maroon, Frilford Grey/Black, Chartreuse Yellow/Black.

ENGINE: Six-cylinder, OHV, bore 79.375mm, stroke 88.9mm, 2639cc (161in³), maximum bhp 101 at 4750rpm, two SU H4 carburettors.

GEARBOX: Four-speed, floor-mounted on right hand side of driver's seat, synchromesh on top three gears. Ratios: top 3.90, 3rd 5.60, 2nd 8.03, 1st 12.93, reverse 17.52.

REAR AXLE: Hypoid bevel, three quarter floating. Ratio 3.89:1.

BRAKES: Lockheed, power assisted, front 11.125in drums, rear 11in drums.

STEERING: Bishop cam and lever.

TYRES: 6.70 x 15.

SUSPENSION: Front, torsion bar, wishbones and links, rear, semi-elliptic leaf springs, telescopic hydraulic dampers front and rear.

DIMENSIONS: Length 15ft 5.5in (4.71m); width 5ft 7in (1.702m); height 5ft 2in (1.57 m); wheelbase 9ft 5.5in (2.883m); track front 4ft 6.375in (1.381m); rear 4ft 6.5in (1.384m); ground clearance 6.5in (16.5cm); turning circle 37ft 5in (11.43m). Approximate weight 1ton, 2cwt, 1qtr, (1635kg).

CAPACITIES: Fuel 13 gallons (59 litres). Boot 11ft³ (0.3m³).

Riley One-Point-Five mark 1

The One-Point-Five or, as it is sometimes called, the 1.5, was introduced in November 1957, a few months after its counterpart the Wolseley Fifteen Hundred. Initially, a replacement for the Morris Minor designed by Alec Issigonis had been considered, using some existing components from that car, but the new Wolseley and Riley models were subsequently produced as a separate range, with larger engines to complement the Minor. There was only one model available for the 1.5, whereas its Wolseley counterpart was available as a Family or Fleet model, the latter having less equipment. The BMC 'B' series engine used in the 1.5 was also used in the Riley 4/68, which, like the 1.5's replacement, the Kestrel, had styling influenced by the Italian company Pininfarina. Standard equipment included water temperature and oil pressure gauges, tachometer (revolution counter), wood-trimmed facia and door cappings, glovebox, leather seats, adjustable individual front bucket seats, two sunvisors, anti-glare mirror, heater, opening front door quarter lights, over-riders, reversing light, and more. Optional equipment included a radio, windscreen washers (standard on later cars), and Duotone paint scheme.

COLOURS: Black, Yukon Grey, Birch Grey, Damask Red, Leaf Green, Florentine Blue. Duotones, main body colour first, Black/Birch Grey, Yukon Grey/Birch Grey, Black/Chartreuse Yellow, Damask Red/Kashmir Beige, and the following with Old English White upper half, Leaf Green, Damask Red, Florentine Blue.

ENGINE: Four-cylinder, OHV, bore 73.02mm, stroke 88.9mm, 1489cc (90.88in^3), maximum bhp 66.5 at 5200rpm, two SU H4 carburettors.

GEARBOX: Four-speed, floor-mounted gear change, synchromesh on top three gears. Ratios: top 3.73, 3rd 5.12, 2nd 8.25, 1st 13.56; reverse 17.73.

REAR AXLE: Hypoid bevel, three quarter floating, ratio 3.73:1.

BRAKES: Girling, front 9in and rear 8in drums, hand brake between front seats.

STEERING: Rack and pinion.
TYRES: 5.00 x 14, from April 1959
5.60 x 14.
SUSPENSION: Front, torsion bars
with vernier adjustment, swivel pins,
rear, semi-elliptic leaf springs, lever
arm shock absorbers front and rear,
note some vehicles may have been
fitted with rear anti-roll bar and
telescopic shock absorbers, instead
of lever arm type to improve handling
characteristics.
DIMENSIONS: Length 12ft 9in
(3.88m); width 5ft 1in (1.55m); height
4ft 11in (1.5m); wheelbase 7ft 2in (2.184m);
track front 4ft 2.9in (1.293m); rear 4ft 2.3in
(1.278m); ground clearance 6.5in (16.5cm);
turning circle 34ft 3in (10.44m); weight (as per
brochure) 18cwt 3qtr 4lb (954kg).
CAPACITIES: Fuel 7 gallons (32 litres). Boot
12.5ft^3 (0.32m^3). Note early brochure quotes
11ft^3 (0.311m^3)

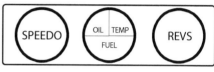

Instrument layout.

Riley One-Point-Five mark 2

Introduced in May 1960 to replace the mark
1 model, the One-Point-Five now had hidden
bonnet and boot hinges, and a full width front
parcel tray. Few changes were made during its
life, and unlike the Wolseley Fifteen Hundred
it retained the same style of Duotone paint
scheme throughout its entire production,
from mark 1 to mark 3. Standard equipment
included water temperature and oil pressure
gauges, tachometer (revolution counter), wood
trimmed facia and door cappings, glovebox,
front parcel shelf, two-tone leather seats,
adjustable individual front bucket seats, two
sunvisors, anti-glare mirror, heater, opening
front door quarter lights, windscreen washers,
over-riders, reversing light and more. Optional
equipment included a radio and Duotone paint
scheme.

COLOURS (1960): Black, Yukon Grey, Birch
Grey, Damask Red, Cumberland Green,
Florentine Blue. Duotones, main body colour
first, Black/Birch Grey, Yukon Grey/Birch Grey,
Black/Chartreuse Yellow, Damask Red/Kashmir
Beige, and the following with Old English White
upper half: Cumberland Green, Damask Red,
Florentine Blue.

ENGINE: Four-cylinder, OHV, bore 73.02mm,
stroke 88.9mm, 1489cc, (90.88in^3),
maximum bhp 66.5 at 5200rpm, two SU H4
carburettors.
GEARBOX: Four-speed, floor-mounted gear
change, synchromesh on top three gears.
Ratios: top 3.73, 3rd 5.12, 2nd 8.25, 1st
13.56, reverse 17.73.
REAR AXLE: Hypoid bevel, three quarter
floating, ratio 3.73:1
BRAKES: Girling, front 9in and rear 8in drums,
hand brake between front seat.
STEERING: Rack and pinion.
TYRES: 5.60 x 14.
SUSPENSION: Front, torsion bars with vernier
adjustment, swivel pins, rear, semi-elliptic leaf
springs, lever arm shock absorbers front & rear.

DIMENSIONS: Length 12ft 9in (3.88m); width 5ft 1in (1.55m); height 5ft (1.52m); wheelbase 7ft 2in (2.184m); track front 4ft 2.9in (1.293m); rear 4ft 2.3in (1.278m); ground clearance 6.5in (16.5cm); turning circle 34ft 3in (10.44m); weight 18cwt 3qtr 4lb (954kg). **CAPACITIES:** Fuel 7 gallons (32 litres). Boot 12.5ft^3 (0.32m^3).

Gear change diagram.

Riley One-Point-Five mark 3

Introduced in October 1961 to replace the mark 2 model, and discontinued in April 1965, the One-Point-Five mark 3 had revised front and rear lights. The front lights became a single unit incorporating indicators and side lights instead of the separate units of previous models, and the rear lights were now of a larger size. There was also a slight change to the front decorative trim to incorporate the new front lights. Standard equipment included water temperature and oil pressure gauges, tachometer (revolution counter), wood-trimmed facia and door cappings, glovebox, front parcel shelf, two-tone leather seats, adjustable individual front bucket seats, two sunvisors, anti-glare mirror, heater, opening front door quarter lights, windscreen washers, over-riders, reversing light, and more. Optional equipment available from car dealerships included a radio, fog and long-range driving lights, wing mirrors, seat belts, anti-mist rear windscreen panel (a popular accessory before heated rear windows became standard equipment).

Number produced all 1.5 models: 39,568.

COLOURS (1960): Black, Dove Grey, Damask Red, Aquamarine, Island Green, Old English White, Florentine Blue, Bermuda Blue. Duotones, main body colour first, Arianca Beige/Pale Ivory, Florentine Blue/Bermuda Blue, Aquamarine/Old English White.

ENGINE: Four-cylinder, OHV, bore 73.02mm, stroke 88.9mm, 1489cc, (90.88in^3), maximum bhp 66.5 at 5200rpm, two SU H4 carburettors.

GEARBOX: Four-speed, floor-mounted gear change, synchromesh on top three gears. Ratios: top 3.73, 3rd 5.12, 2nd 8.25, 1st 13.56, reverse 17.73

REAR AXLE: Hypoid bevel, three quarter floating, ratio 3.73:1.

BRAKES: Girling, front 9in and rear 8in drums, hand brake between front seat.

STEERING: Rack and pinion.

TYRES: 5.60 x 14.

SUSPENSION: Front, torsion bars with vernier adjustment, swivel pins, rear, semi-elliptic leaf springs, lever arm shock absorbers front and rear.

DIMENSIONS: Length 12ft 9in (3.88m);

width 5ft 1in (1.55m); height 4ft 11in (1.5m); wheelbase 7ft 2in (2.184m); track front 4ft 2.9in (1.293m); rear 4ft 2.3in (1.278m); ground clearance 6.5in (16.5cm); turning circle 34ft 3in (10.44m); weight 18cwt 3qtr 4lb (954kg). **CAPACITIES:** Fuel 7 gallons (32 litres). Boot 12.5ft^3 (0.32m^3).

Left: The One-Point-Five mark 1 and 2; right: mark 3. Note different front grille and side lights/ indicators.

Riley Elf mark 1

Introduced in October 1961 (the same time as the Riley 4/Seventy Two), the Elf was, in effect, a luxury Mini with an extended boot. It had a central oval instrument panel with the speedometer in the middle, oil pressure and water temperature gauges on each side, and a wood-trimmed surround. Additional equipment included a heater and bonnet lock as standard. The front grille, however, was attached to the bonnet, making it more difficult when working on the engine or simply checking the oil level. The rear boot lid also came in for criticism as it was hinged at the top and liable to fall down. This was first ever front-wheel drive Riley, and the only substantial change during its lifetime was the fitting of an engine of greater cubic capacity. Standard equipment included water temperature and oil pressure gauges, walnut trimmed instrument panel, heater, hinged opening rear quarter lights, sliding/opening front windows, leather seats, parcel shelves each side of the instrument panel, large front door bins, cubby box with ashtray either side of rear seat, protective door kick plates, windscreen washers, and wheel embellishers. Optional equipment included radio, seatbelts, wing mirrors, fog, spot and reversing lights.
Number produced: all Elf models, approximately 30,900.
Price when introduced: £694.

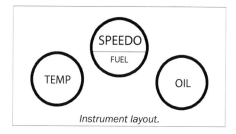

Instrument layout.

COLOURS: Main body colour first, second is roof colour, Florentine Blue/Chartreuse Yellow, Whitehall Beige/Damask Red, Birch Grey/Yukon Grey; all the following with Old English White roof, Cumberland Green, Florentine Blue, Birch Grey
ENGINE: Four-cylinder, OHV, bore 62.94mm, stroke 68.26mm, 848cc (51.8in^3), maximum bhp 34 at 5500rpm, single SU HS2 carburettor.
GEARBOX: Four-speed, floor-mounted gear change, synchromesh on top three gears. Ratios: top 3.765, 3rd 5.317, 2nd 8.176, 1st 13.657. Front-wheel drive with helical spur gears and open drive shafts with universal joints, final drive ratio 3.765:1.
BRAKES: Lockheed front and rear 7in drums, with handbrake between the front seats.

STEERING: Rack and pinion.
TYRES: 5.20 x 10.
SUSPENSION: Front independent with upper and lower suspension arms, rear trailing arms, with Moulton rubber cone springs and hydraulic telescopic shock absorbers front and rear.
DIMENSIONS: Length 10ft 8.75in (3.27m); width 4ft 7in (1.397m); height 4ft 5in (1.346m); wheelbase 6ft 8in (2.03m); track front 3ft 11.437in (1.198m); rear 3ft 9.875in (1.164m); ground clearance 6.375in (16.1cm); turning circle 30ft (9.4m). Note all information above taken from brochures.
CAPACITIES: Fuel 5.5 gallons (25 litres). Boot 6ft^3 (0.17m^3).

Riley Elf mark 2

Introduced in March 1963 with an enlarged engine of 998cc, achieved by increasing both the bore and stroke, it only gained an extra 4bhp. Externally, only a mark 2 badge on the boot lid differentiated it from the mark 1. The boot lid was now counterbalanced to offset complaints about it not staying open (not a problem experienced with the Austin and Morris Minis, whose boot lids were hinged at the bottom so they simply stayed down when open). Other changes over the mark 1 included replacing the open parcel shelves on each side of the instrument panel with gloveboxes with lids, and improvements included the fitting of wider front brake drums, now 1.5in instead of 1.25in. In September 1964 a new diaphragm spring clutch was fitted, and Hydrolastic suspension replaced the rubber cone suspension of earlier cars. Standard equipment included water temperature and oil pressure gauges, walnut trimmed instrument panel, heater, leather seats, two gloveboxes, large front door bins, cubby box with ashtray either side of rear seat, protective door kick plates, windscreen washers, and carpeted boot, over-riders. Optional equipment included a radio, reclining front seats, seatbelts, electrically heated rear window, and wing mirrors.

COLOURS: Main body colour first, second is roof colour, Florentine Blue/Chartreuse Yellow, Whitehall Beige/Damask Red, Birch Grey/ Yukon Grey; all the following with Old English

White roof, Cumberland Green, Florentine Blue, Birch Grey.
ENGINE: Four-cylinder, OHV, bore 64.58mm, stroke 76.2mm, 998cc (60.96in³), maximum bhp 38 at 5200rpm, single SU HS2 carburettor. Note the new 998cc engine was derived from the 1100 models engine rather than being a development of the original 848cc unit.
GEARBOX: Four-speed, floor-mounted gear change, synchromesh on top three gears. Ratios: top 3.765, 3rd 5.317, 2nd 8.176, 1st 13.657, reverse 13.657. Front-wheel drive with helical spur gears and open drive shafts with universal joints, final drive ratio 3.765:1.
BRAKES: Lockheed front and rear 7in drums, with two leading shoes for front brakes.
STEERING: Rack and pinion.
TYRES: 5.20 x 10.
SUSPENSION: Front independent with upper and lower suspension arms, rear trailing arms, with rubber cone springs and telescopic shock absorbers (mark 1 and early mark 2), then from 1964 interconnected Hydrolastic displacers replaced the rubber cone suspension (later mark 2 and all mark 3 models).
DIMENSIONS: 10ft 10.31in (3.31m); width 4ft 7.5in (1.40m); height 4ft 5in (1.346m); wheelbase 6ft 8.16in (2.04m); track front 3ft 11.437in (1.20m); rear 3ft 9.875in (1.16m);

Austin/Morris Mini had simpler rear styling than the Riley Elf.

A self adhesive heated rear window panel, a popular accessory before heated rear windows became standard equipment.

ground clearance 6.125in (1.56cm); turning circle 31ft 7in (9.63m); approximate weight 13cwt (665kg).
CAPACITIES: Fuel, 5.5 gallons (25 litres).

Riley Elf mark 3

Introduced in October 1966, the mark 3 was restyled with hidden door hinges and wind-down front windows. On the inside new features included a remote floor gear change, and a multi purpose stalk on the steering column, controlling indicators, horn, headlight flasher and high/low beam. The Elf was discontinued in 1969 at the same time as the rest of the Riley range. Standard equipment included water temperature and oil pressure gauges, walnut-trimmed instrument panel, heater, leather seats, front door bins (revised for mark 3 as a result of the fitting of wind-down windows), cubby box with ashtray on each side of rear seat, protective door kick plates, windscreen washers, carpeted boot, wheel embellishers, and over-riders. Optional equipment included a radio, reclining front seats, seatbelts, electrically heated rear window, wing mirrors, and automatic transmission.

Price in 1966: £647.

COLOURS (1968): Body colour first, followed by roof colour: Faun Brown/Pale Ivory, Damask Red/Whitehall Beige; the following came with a Snowberry White roof: Cumberland Green, Persian Blue, Birch Grey, Yukon Grey, single tone Snowberry White body and roof.

ENGINE: Four-cylinder, OHV, bore 64.58mm, stroke 76.2mm, 998cc (60.89in^3), maximum bhp 38, single SU HS2 carburettor.

GEARBOX: Four-speed, floor-mounted gear change, synchromesh on top three gears for the early cars, and synchromesh on all forward gears on the later cars. Ratios with manual gearbox: top 3.765, 3rd 5.317, 2nd 8.176, 1st 13.657, reverse 13.657. Front-wheel drive with helical spur gears and open drive shafts with

universal joints, final drive ratio manual and automatic: 3.765:1.
BRAKES: Lockheed front and rear 7in drums.
STEERING: Rack and pinion.
TYRES: 5.20 x 10, note spare wheel for all the Elf models was in a recess under the rear boot carpet, requiring the entire contents of the boot to be removed before it could be accessed; the battery was also under the boot floor carpet.
SUSPENSION: Front independent with upper and lower suspension arms, rear trailing arms with interconnected Hydrolastic displacers front and rear.
DIMENSIONS: Length 10ft 10.31in (3.31m); width 4ft 7.5in (1.40m); height 4ft 5in (1.346m); wheelbase 6ft 8.16in (2.04m); track front 3ft 11.437 (1.20m), 3ft 9.875in (1.16m); ground clearance 6.125in (1.56cm); turning circle 31ft 7in (9.63m); approximate weight 13cwt (665kg).
CAPACITIES: Fuel 5.5 gallons (25 litres). Boot 6ft³ (0.17m³).

Gear change diagram.

The badges on the boot lid identify this as a mark 3. Unlike the Austin/Morris Mini there were no styling changes to the rear of the car during its lifetime.

Riley Kestrel 1100

Introduced in September 1965 at the same time as the Wolseley 1100, and several years after the Austin and Morris 1100 models, the Kestrel was intended to fill the space in the Riley range that had become

A Kestrel 1100 mark 1.

vacant following the discontinuation of the One-Point-Five in April 1965. The Kestrel name had previously been used for another Riley car in the 1930s but the new Kestrel was simply an upmarket version of the Austin/Morris 1100, and generally had the same equipment levels as the MG and Wolseley models but it was the only 1100 in the BMC range to feature circular dials instead of the ribbon type used in the other variants. It also was the only model fitted with a revolution counter. It was fitted with Hydrolastic suspension which consisted of interconnected front and rear displacer units on each side, which, when a wheel passes over an uneven surface, causes rubber cups in the unit to come together squeezing fluid along pipes to the opposite end of the car keeping the car level and eliminating the bounce effect associated with conventional springs. The spare wheel was under a panel in the boot, requiring all luggage to be removed to access it. It was only available as a four-door saloon unlike some of the other BMC models that were available as two-door saloons and estates. The 1275cc engine was offered as an option in June 1967, and cars fitted with this engine were called the Riley Kestrel 1275. Then, in October 1967, the 1300 model was introduced as a separate variant and the 1100 became the mark 2 model, which featured revised rear lights and modified rear wings and repeater indicators on the front wings it had a relatively short life and was discontinued in 1968 at which point the 1300 became the mark 2 model. Standard equipment in 1965 included, heater, revolution counter, water temperature and oil pressure gauges, veneered walnut

facia panel, large front door bins, leather trimmed seats, opening front quarter lights, windscreen washers, headlight flasher, bonnet lock operated from inside car, front seatbelt fixing points, over-riders and more. Optional extras included radio, whitewall tyres. Dealer fitted options included wing mirrors, fog lights, locking petrol cap, anti-mist rear window panel, a popular accessory before heated rear windows were fitted as standard equipment.

COLOURS (1965): Single tone, Snowberry White, Sandy Beige, Aquamarine, Agate Red, Cumberland Green, Black. Duotones, main body colour first, Snowberry White/Sandy Beige, Snowberry White/Cumberland Green, Sandy Beige/Arianca Beige, Aquamarine/Snowberry White.

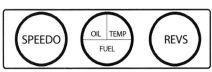

Instrument layout.

ENGINE: Four-cylinder, OHV, bore 64.58mm, stroke 83.72mm, 1098cc (67.02in^3), maximum bhp 55 at 5500rpm, two SU HS2 carburettors. For 1275 details see 1300.

GEARBOX (mark 1): Four-speed, floor-mounted gear change, synchromesh on top three gears. Ratios: top 4.133, 3rd 5.83, 2nd 8.98, 1st 14.99, reverse 14.99. Front-wheel drive by spur gears and drive shafts with velocity joints, final drive ratio mark 1, 4.133:1.

BRAKES: Lockheed with pressure limiting valve fitted to apportion more accurately braking between front and rear wheels, front 8in discs and rear 8in drums.

STEERING: Rack and pinion.

TYRES: 5.50 x 12.

SUSPENSION: Front independent wishbone, rear independent trailing arms and anti-roll bar, front and rear interconnected Hydrolastic displacers.

DIMENSIONS: Length 12ft 2.75in (3.73m); width 5ft 0.4in (1.534m); height 4ft 4.75in (1.34m); wheelbase 7ft 9.5in (2.375m); track front 4ft 3.5in (1.308m); rear 4ft 2.9in (1.292m); ground clearance 6.125in (15.6cm); turning circle 34ft (10.363m); approximate

weight 16cwt 2qtr 21lb (849kg).
CAPACITIES: Fuel tank 8 gallons (36 litres).
Boot 9.5ft^3 (0.269m^3).

Gear change diagram.

The car above is an 1100 mark 2.

Riley Kestrel 1300

Introduced in October 1967 as a separate model these cars were fitted with an all synchromesh gearbox and replaced the Riley Kestrel 1275, then in October 1968 the 1300 became the mark 2 and was fitted with a more powerful engine and revised gearbox, it was subsequently discontinued in 1969 along with the other remaining Riley models. Other changes in October 1968 included the restyling of the rear with number plate lights being on fitted on the boot lid instead of the bumper, the Kestrel name was

Kestrel 1300 mark 1 which has been painted in the same style as the MG models.

91

deleted and the Duotone paint scheme was no longer available. Standard equipment for the Riley Kestrel 1300 included heater, revolution counter, water temperature and oil pressure gauges, veneered walnut facia panel, large front door bins, leather trimmed seats, opening front quarter lights, windscreen washers and single lever on the steering column operated the headlight flasher, dip-switch, direction indicators, horn. For the Riley 1300 mark 2 rouched door pockets replaced the door bins, a smaller steering wheel was fitted and rocker switches replaced the earlier toggle type. Optional factory fitted items included, reclining front seats, heated rear window and automatic transmission. Dealer fitted items such as radio and seatbelts incurred a separate fitting charge in addition to the price of the item.

COLOURS (1969): Single tones only, Snowberry White, Connaught Green, Bermuda Blue, Trafalgar Blue, Cumulus Grey, Faun Brown, Sandy Beige, Damask Red.
ENGINE 1275 and 1300: Four-cylinder, OHV, bore 70.61mm, stroke 81.28mm, 1275cc (77.82in³). 1275 and 1300 mark 1 manual and automatics, maximum bhp 58 at 5250rpm, single SU HS4 carburettor. 1300

The car above is a Riley Kestrel 1300 mark 1. The blue car below is a mark 2.

Left, the mark 2 did not have the Kestrel name on the boot.

mark 2 maximum bhp 70 at 6000rpm, two SU HS2 carburettors.

GEARBOX: Four-speed, floor-mounted gear change, 1275 synchromesh on top three gears, top 3.65, 3rd 5.16, 2nd 7.95, 1st 13.23. 1300 synchromesh on all gears. Ratios: vary according to source, and for mark 1 are sometimes quoted as top 3.65, 3rd 5.61, 2nd 7.92, 1st 13.21, reverse 13.21 and top 3.65, 3rd 5.22, 2nd 8.3, 1st 12.85, reverse 12.85. For the 1300 mark 2, top 3.65, 3rd 4.93, 2nd 7.57, 1st 12.04, reverse 12.22, all with front-wheel drive with Helical spur gears and open drive shafts with universal joints. Final drive ratio manual gearbox 3.65:1.

BRAKES: Lockheed with pressure limiting valve fitted to apportion more accurately braking between front and rear wheels, front 8.39in discs and rear 8in drums. Note early cars had 8in front discs.

STEERING: Rack and pinion.

TYRES: 5.50 x 12.

SUSPENSION: Front independent wishbone, rear independent trailing arms and anti-roll bar, front and rear interconnected Hydrolastic displacers.

DIMENSIONS: Length 12ft 2.75in (3.73m); width 5ft 0.4in (1.534m); height 4ft 4.75in (1.34m); wheelbase 7ft 9.5in (2.375m); track front 4ft 3.5in (1.308m); rear 4ft

2.9in (1.292m); ground clearance 6.125in (15.6cm); turning circle 34ft (10.363m); approximate weight 16cwt 2qtr 21lb (849kg).

CAPACITIES: Fuel tank 8 gallons (36 litres). Boot 9.5ft^3 (0.269m^3).

Riley (top), Wolseley (middle), and MG (bottom) all featured different styles of Duotone paint schemes, but models of all makes after October 1968 were only available with single colours.

Riley 1300 mark 2.

Riley 4/Sixty Eight (4/68)

Introduced in April 1959, the 4/68 was one of the BMC Farina cars. However, unlike its Austin and Morris counterparts, there was never an estate variant. The Austin, Morris and Wolseley cars all had pointed tail fins, a popular styling feature of 1950s cars; however, the MG and Riley models had the less pronounced shorter tail fins from the start. A special edition produced by Wessex Motors of Salisbury, called the Riley Riviera and painted in Royal Blue, featured a restyled rear end, wire wheels, and the MGA 1588cc engine. Standard equipment for the 4/68 included water temperature and oil pressure gauges, ammeter, tachometer, clock, two sunvisors, lockable glovebox, front parcel shelf, separate bucket style front seats with individual adjustment, a folding centre armrest in the rear seat and armrests on rear doors, windscreen washers, opening quarter lights, reversing lights, and over-riders. Optional equipment included heater and radio. **Number produced:** Approximately 10,400.

COLOURS (1960): Black, Leaf Green, Birch Grey, Damask Red, Old English White. Duotones, roof and boot lid first, Yukon Grey/

Close up of extra trim required for Duotone paint scheme.

Wheel trim: the wheels on this car are painted in same colour as the main body.

Birch Grey, Damask Red/Old English White,
Connaught Green/Leaf Green, Leaf Green/Old
English White.
ENGINE: Four-cylinder, OHV, bore 73.025mm,
stroke 88.9mm, 1489cc (90.88in³), maximum
bhp 66.5 at 5200, two SU HD4 carburettors.
GEARBOX: Four-speed, floor-mounted gear
change, synchromesh on top three gears.
Ratios: top 4.30, 3rd 5.91, 2nd 9.52, 1st
15.64, reverse 20.45.
REAR AXLE: Hypoid bevel, three quarter
floating*, ratio 4.30:1.
BRAKES: Girling, front and rear 9in drums,
handbrake between driver's seat and door.
STEERING: Cam and peg.
TYRES: 5.90 x 14, spare wheel in tray
underneath the rear of the car.
SUSPENSION: Front, coil spring and wishbone,
rear semi-elliptic leaf springs, telescopic shock
absorbers front and rear.
DIMENSIONS: Length 14ft 10.1in (4.52m);
width 5ft 3.5in (1.61m); height 4ft 11.75in
(1.52m); wheelbase 8ft 3.2in (2.52m); track
front 4ft 0.56in (1.23m)*; rear 4ft 1.875in
(1.267m)*; ground clearance 6.5in (16.5cm);
turning circle 37ft 6in (11.43m)
CAPACITIES: Fuel 10 gallons (45 litres). Boot
19ft³ (0.538m³).
* As per brochure.

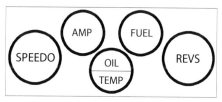

Instrument layout.

Gear change
layout.

The special edition 4/68 – the Riley Riviera.

Riley 4/Seventy Two (4/72)

Introduced in October 1961 to replace the 4/68, the 4/72 had a larger engine and changes to overall length, wheelbase and track. Unlike the rest of the BMC Farina range it retained its original styling which featured 'cropped' rear tail fins from the start. The Duotone body colours changed from the 4/68 models, and were now split in a simpler style, with the complete top half of the car painted one colour and the lower half painted another, with a chrome strip running along the side and across the boot lid to separate the two colours. Changes during its

lifetime included modifying the suspension and steering, elimination of some greasing points. The Riley 4/72 was discontinued in 1968. Standard equipment in 1961 included: water temperature and oil pressure gauges, ammeter, tachometer (revolution counter), clock, heater, two sunvisors, lockable glovebox, front parcel shelf, wood veneer facia and door cappings, separate front seats with individual adjustment, folding centre armrest in rear seat and armrests on rear doors, reversing lights, and over-riders. Optional extras included screen washers (standard equipment from 1962), automatic transmission, radio, wing mirrors, and seatbelts.

Number produced: Approximately 14,150.

COLOURS (1961): Single tones, Black, Dove Grey, Arianca Beige, Maroon, Iris Blue, Almond Green. Duotones, top colour first, Arianca Beige/Sandy Beige, Almond Green/ Porcelain Green, Dove Grey/Old English White, Iris Blue/Old English White.
ENGINE: Four-cylinder, OHV, bore 76.2mm, stroke 88.9mm, 1622cc (98.94in³), maximum bhp 68 at 5000, two SU HD4 carburettors.
GEARBOX: Four-speed, floor-mounted gear change, synchromesh on top three gears.

Ratios: top 4.30, 3rd 5.91, 2nd 9.52, 1st 15.64, reverse 20.45.
REAR AXLE: Hypoid bevel, three quarter

floating, ratio 4.30:1.
BRAKES: Girling, front and rear 9in drums, handbrake between driver's seat and door.
STEERING: Cam and peg.
TYRES: 5.90 x 14, spare wheel in tray under boot floor.
SUSPENSION: Front, coil spring and wishbone, rear semi-elliptic leaf springs with telescopic shock absorbers and anti-roll bars front and rear.

DIMENSIONS: Length 14ft 10.25in (4.52m); width 5ft 3.5in (1.61m); height 4ft 10.25in (1.48m); wheelbase 8ft 4.25in (2.55m); track front 4ft 2.563in (1.28m); rear 4ft 3.75in (1.3m); ground clearance 6.5in (16.5cm); turning circle 37ft (11.28m); weight approximately 1ton 2cwt (1118kg).
CAPACITIES: Fuel 10 gallons (45 litres). Boot 19ft³ (0.538m³).

Rear light arrangements. Top row, left to right: Riley 4/68, MG Magnette mark 3, Austin Cambridge A55, Morris Oxford mark 5, Wolseley 15/60. Bottom row: Riley 4/72, MG Magnette mark 4, Austin Cambridge A60, Morris Oxford mark 6, Wolseley 16/60.

More in the Pictorial History series:

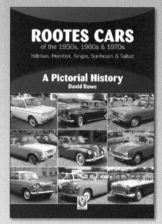

ISBN: 978-1-787114-43-2

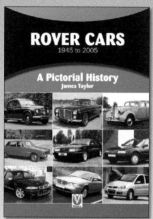

ISBN: 978-1-787116-09-2

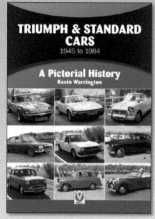

ISBN: 978-1-787110-77-9

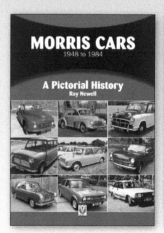

ISBN: 978-1-787110-55-7

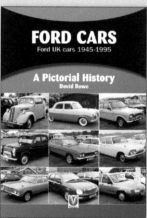

ISBN: 978-1-787116-42-9

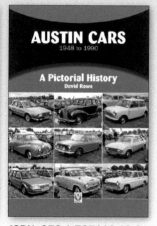

ISBN: 978-1-787112-19-3

The ultimate guides to these classic marques. Ideal for the enthusiast or collector, or for those who enjoy a trip down memory lane. The books cover every model of the period, are packed with full model specs, interesting facts, and fully illustrated in colour. See the full range on the Veloce website, more titles coming soon!

More from Veloce Publishing:

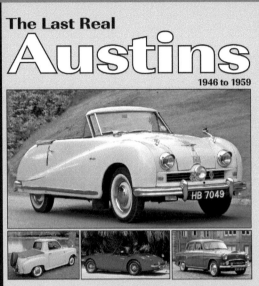

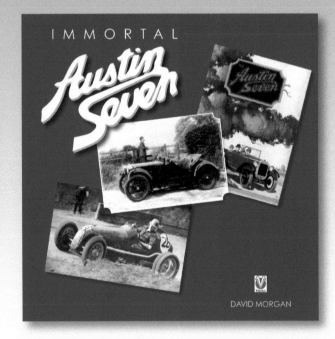

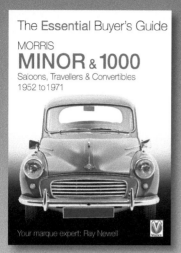

The Essential Buyer's Guide

MORRIS
MINOR & 1000
Saloons, Travellers & Convertibles
1952 to 1971

Your marque expert: Ray Newell

ISBN: 978-1-845841-01-0
Paperback • 19.5x13.9cm
• 64 pages • 158 pictures

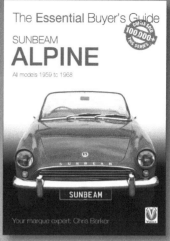

The Essential Buyer's Guide

SUNBEAM
ALPINE
All models 1959 to 1968

Your marque expert: Chris Barker

SUNBEAM

ISBN: 978-1-845849-25-2
Paperback • 19.5x13.9cm
• 64 pages • 100 pictures

The Essential Buyer's Guide

MG & AUSTIN-HEALEY
MIDGET
& SPRITE
All models 1958 to 1979

Your marque expert: Terry Horler

ISBN: 978-1-787114-21-0
Paperback • 19.5x13.9cm
• 64 pages • 99 pictures

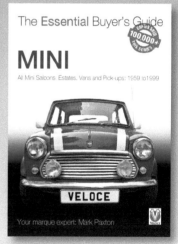

The Essential Buyer's Guide

MINI
All Mini Saloons, Estates, Vans and Pick-ups: 1959 to1999

Your marque expert: Mark Paxton

VELOCE

ISBN: 978-1-84584-204-8
Paperback • 19.5x13.9cm
• 64 pages • 103 pictures

The Essential Buyer's Guide series:

Having one of these books in your pocket is just like having a real marque expert by your side. Benefit from the author's experience, learn how to spot a bad car quickly and how to assess a promising one like a professional. Get the right car at the right price!

- ◆ Now over 100 titles in this best-selling series
- ◆ Many also available as eBooks – see www.digital.veloce.co.uk

For more information and price details, visit our website at www.veloce.co.uk

GREAT CARS

Veloce *Classic Reprint* Series

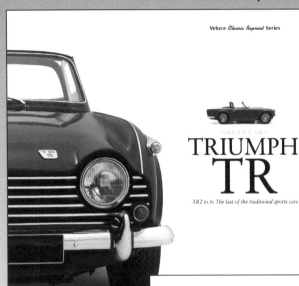

The Triumph TR range has earned its place among the most popular sports cars of all time, with enthusiasts and owners on both sides of the Atlantic. The cars covered here range from the original, basic, four-cylinder TR2 of 1953, to the hairy-chested six-cylinder TR6 that finally bowed out of production in 1975, replaced by the unloved TR7.

ISBN: 978-1-845848-54-5
Hardback • 25x25cm
• 160 pages • 295 pictures

The Austin Healey – or 'Big' Healey – is one of the most iconic British sports cars. The first Austin-Healey 100 model was unveiled at the 1952 Earls Court Motor Show, and when the last car rolled off the production line in 1967, over 73,000 examples had been built.

ISBN: 978-1-845848-55-2
Hardback • 25x25cm
• 160 pages • 270 pictures

LOOK OUT FOR MORE *GREAT CARS* IN THIS SERIES

email: info@veloce.co.uk • Tel: +44(0)1305 260068

INDEX

www.veloce.co.uk / www.velocebooks.com
All current books • new book news • Special offers • Gift vouchers